How to

PASS

Accounting
Exams

Simon Parry

CONTENTS

INTRODUCTION

What Will You Gain from This Book?

In this book you will learn how to become better at passing accounting exams. You will learn how to use your study time more effectively and efficiently and how to translate your efforts into better marks in the exam.

There are no secrets to achieving this. Success in passing accounting exams is dependent upon two key factors:
*   good preparation before the exam, and
*   good performance in the exam

Obvious, you may think. But what is not so obvious to many students is that these are two different sets of skills. Both are important. Both can be improved – and improved dramatically.

It is not difficult to become a more effective student. You just need to know how. You are about to learn.

Why I Am Qualified to Write This Book?

A reasonable question to ask of anyone claiming expertise in how to pass accounting exams is "what are your credentials?"

This book is born out of a long career in accounting education. I have spent over 20 years as an accounting tutor, and I have been an examiner for several professional bodies and academic institutions.

I have coached thousands of students through accounting exams, ranging from basic accounting and book-keeping courses to university degree courses, postgraduate Masters courses, and professional accounting exams.

During this time, I have gained considerable insight into the examination process. I have been writing and marking exam papers for professional accounting bodies and universities for 20 years. I was the ACCA Chief External Examiner for 5 years, and before that I sat on the ICAEW Exam Review Board. I have been an external examiner for several universities worldwide, both at undergraduate and post-graduate level. I have been an ACCA exam marker on 5 different papers. Through this experience I have seen tens of thousands of accounting exam scripts. These include the good, the bad and the ugly.

For much of my career as an accounting tutor I have supported students through professional accounting exams, namely ACCA , CIMA and ICAEW. Some of these exams have global pass rates of only 35 – 40% - that's right, over 60% of the students sitting the exam fail. Among my students the pass rate has consistently been 90%+, and on many occasions 100% of my students have passed. I therefore KNOW that what I am about to share with you REALLY WORKS.

And of course, I practice what I preach. I have sat

and passed several accounting exams myself. I am a Fellow of the Institute of Chartered Accountants in England and Wales, having passed my professional exams with that body. I also have an MBA and a PhD in accounting. I know from first-hand experience what it feels like to have to prepare for and sit accounting exams.

My motivation for writing this book has been a desire to see more accounting students succeed. As an examiner, it is heart breaking to fail an exam script when you know that behind that script lies all the hard work, hopes and aspirations of its author. But, as any examiner will tell you, marks can only be awarded for what is actually written on the answer script. This book is my attempt at helping you to ensure that what the examiner reads on your answer script will get you a pass.

PART 1:

EFFECTIVE EXAM PREPARATION

This book is divided into two parts. This first part covers what you should do between now and going into the examination hall. It is about preparing yourself for the exam. The second part is about what you should do when you are in the examination hall. It is about exam technique.

Exam success is about getting both of these right. In order to pass you need good preparation prior to the exam and good performance on the day.

These are two separate aspects to exam success and to a large extent, two separate sets of skills. This is why I have separated them out into two sections. Both are important and you need to work on improving both sets of skills to increase your chances of passing your exams.

So, let's get started on the first set of skills – let's look at how you can improve the way you prepare for your exams.

.

CHAPTER 1:
MAKE SPACE FOR YOUR STUDIES

It should be obvious that you are going to struggle to perform well in the exam if you have not prepared yourself adequately beforehand.

Unfortunately, too many students do fail to prepare adequately. They bury their head in the sand and tell themselves "it will be alright on the night".

In my experience it is often the more able students who do this. Students who are very bright and learn quickly are quite often able to succeed in school without too much effort. They therefore fall into a habit of inadequate preparation, because that has always worked for them in the past.

The problem is that accounting exams are difficult. They can require a lot of detailed technical knowledge that is not common sense. You need to learn many theories, models and techniques. If you go into the exam without adequate preparation you WILL fail. Thousands of professional accounting students do so every year. The pass rate in some professional accounting papers can be as low as 30%.

This means that if you want to succeed in the exam you need to put a good action plan in place that will ensure you are adequately prepared. You need to go into the exam with the necessary technical knowledge; you need to have practised exam technique; you need a good understanding of the types of questions you are going to face; and you need to know what the examiner expects of you.

Motivation vs. Commitment

We've all heard motivational speakers. They whip you up into a frenzy of enthusiasm with "can-do" language, high energy and passion. We can all get pumped up about something and find a rush of enthusiasm: jump out of bed at 5am into a cold shower and then hit the studying hard for 2 hours before going to work. The problem is that this is difficult to sustain. Motivation drops off very quickly and we fall back into old habits.

Rather than motivation, you need commitment. Commitment is the resolution to stick to your study plan and make it happen, even when you don't feel motivated. Motivation is great. If you can find and sustain it, good for you. But for most of us it is dogged determination, a real commitment that will get us through.

So, let's start by looking at some of the most important basics of exam preparation that will help you make this commitment. The first and most important step is to make space for your studies. You need both psychological space and physical space to give yourself the best chance of optimising your exam preparation time and effort.

Make Psychological Space

In preparing yourself to pass an accounting exam, your greatest challenge will be psychological. Your biggest enemy will be stress. Therefore, the foundation of good exam preparation is stress management. Throughout this book many of the recommendations I make are aimed at managing and reducing the stress that exam preparation generates.

You must accept, right now, that in the run-up to your exams you are going to have to spend a lot of time studying. What many people refuse to accept is that to make space for all this studying, other things in your life are going to have to be put aside for a short time. If you are involved in other activities - social, sporting, clubs or societies, then you will have to cut back on the time you put into these during your study period to give yourself more time to concentrate on exam preparation.

This does not mean that you must permanently give up your social life and other interests. What is required is a temporary shift in the way you spend your time. It is a short-term investment that will generate a long-term payback. Think about that payback. See beyond the short-term sacrifice to your long-term goals.

I have seen too many students refuse to cut back on other activities and make space for studying. The result has been damaging to their career, and in many cases also ultimately it has meant that they have less time for their other interests, because repeated exam resits have dragged their period of study out for much longer than was necessary.

A student once came to me for private tuition after spending 10 years trying to pass his CIMA exams. All I did was help him organise his life around a systematic and scheduled study timetable. He went on to pass his outstanding exams at the next sitting.

So, before you even start to put together a study plan, make sure that you are approaching this in the right frame of mind. Give it 100% commitment. Embrace this period of intense exam preparation in a positive frame of mind. See it as a positive investment of your time and energy, over a relatively short period of time, that will bring you long-term benefits which vastly outweigh the sacrifices you make.

One very good way of doing this is to promise yourself rewards for your effort. The long-term rewards are of course all the benefits that come from passing your exams. However, those rewards can sometimes seem too distant and remote when you still have several more months or years of studying to complete. You therefore also need rewards for short-term successes throughout your studies. I will give you more tips on this later.

In particular, you should promise yourself a reward that you will receive immediately after you have finished your exams. You can hold this in mind throughout your studies. Every time you don't feel like returning to your studies, remind yourself of the reward you will get if you do.

Paul was one of my ACCA students. He knew that if he passed his exams his employer would reward him with a substantial increase in salary. Paul loved cars and promised himself that he would use the extra money to finance the car he really wanted. He cut a photo of the car from a magazine and pinned it on the wall in his study space. Every time Paul sat down to study, he promised himself that the car was his if he passed.

Katrina was another of my ACCA students. As well as having a busy job, she was a single mother. She promised herself a holiday at Disneyland with her daughter after her exams. She found a postcard of Disneyland and pinned it on the wall of her study space next to a photo of her daughter.

Andre was in one of my CIMA classes. He loved to cook. He invited all his classmates to a barbeque at his home the weekend after the exams. That was his reward, not just to himself, but to the whole class.

What will your reward to yourself be? Write it down and find an inspiring picture. Make yourself a 'reward' poster and either tape it to the front of your study folder or pin it on the wall in your study space.

Make Physical Space

Having prepared yourself psychologically, the next step is to find a place where you can regularly study. If you are living with family or friends, then you need to talk to them and explain that you are going to need time and space to get on with your studying for a limited period. You should explain to them that you would appreciate their help by being quiet when you are studying and in accepting that you will have less time to be sociable with them than you normally would. This may require some good negotiating skills!

Allow for some give and take, but try and get them on your side. It is better to have the willing cooperation of those around you. You may even be able to get them involved with your studying in a way that enables them to actively support and help you. More on this later.

If possible, create a space where you can set up and leave all your study material. If you are able do this, it means that when you have time to study, you can just sit down and pick up where you left off last time, rather than having to get all your books and notes out and set up your study space again. Another advantage of doing this is that you can create mind maps, timetables and work plans and stick them on the wall around your study space.

Not everyone has the luxury of being able to create such a study space in their own home. If this is the case for you, you should try to find some quiet area where you can regularly be undisturbed for one to two hours at a time.

There are several ways you can find such a space:

- There may be a public library or other public building near where you live, where you are able to find a quiet corner to sit and work.

- If you are studying for your exams in a college, the college may be able to provide a quiet workspace or you.

- If you are working, your employer may be happy to let you arrive at work early or stay late and use your workspace or some other place to study.

- If you cannot find a quiet space in your own home, you may be able to find one in a friend's home. If you have a good friend who is willing to support you through your studies, then they may be happy to provide you with the quiet study space you need.

The important thing is that you must find somewhere where you can concentrate on your studies without interruption or distraction.

Chapter Summary

This chapter has looked at the importance of creating the space in your life that is necessary to effective exam preparation.

Most people do not have sufficient space in their life to fit in studying without making other changes. We are all very busy, juggling work, family, household chores, friends and other interests. This means that it is necessary to make changes in order to create this space. You cannot expect to undertake effective exam preparation without making changes in other areas of your life.

Key Points:

The advice in this section may seem very simple and obvious, but it is extremely important. You cannot establish and sustain a structured programme of study without creating both the psychological and physical space in which to do this:

- Prepare yourself psychologically for spending more time on your studying for this limited period.

- Prepare those around you for the fact that you will be less available to them for this limited period. Secure their support.

- Find a physical space where you can concentrate on your studies without distraction.

CHAPTER 2:
GETTING ORGANISED

Make a Study Plan – Now!

When you begin your exam preparation the first thing you should do is to create a study plan. In this chapter I will guide you through the process of creating one.

It is my experience that most students over-estimate how much time they will have available for study. It is better to accept that you are not going to be able to do as much studying as you would like. You must be realistic about how much studying you can achieve before the exam. The key to success is making the most effective use of the time that you do have available.

You should be realistic in putting together a study plan. Intending to study for 14 or 15 hours a day, every day, is not realistic. Even if you were able to find that amount of time, attempting to do so much studying would exhaust you and would be counterproductive. There can be a lot of gung-ho behaviour and caffeine-fuelled all-night studying before exams. I have seen this many times. Believe me, that is not the best way. It is not the most effective strategy and it is certainly not good for your mental or physical wellbeing.

It is much better to have a longer-term, structured, slow-burn approach to exam preparation. This is not just because of your health, but because all the research shows that this is the most effective strategy for exam success.

So, let's look at the steps involved in putting together a winning study plan that will ensure that you arrive at the exam hall well prepared.

Decide How Much Time You Can Dedicate to Study

Your first step in making a study plan should be to decide how much time you can invest in studying. Look realistically at what time you have available but bear in mind the advice I offered in chapter 1: You will need to put other activities aside in order to create time to study.

Let's say you can find 2 hours per day, for 6 days out of each week. That gives you 12 hours per week. Let's also say that it is now 8 weeks until your exam. That gives you a total of 96 hours of study time, split into 48 two-hour sessions.

If you are studying for more than one exam, then you need to decide how you are going to split your time across the different topics that you need to study. This will give you an idea of how much time you have available to concentrate on each exam. Don't just split your time equally between the exams. Follow my advice below in prioritising topics and making sure you use your study time most effectively.

Now that you have created a framework of time slots for your study plan, you need to decide how to fill them.

Prepare an Overview of the Whole Syllabus

In order to decide how to use your study time, start by getting the big picture of what you need to know. Prepare an overview of the whole syllabus. Do this separately for each exam. Produce your overview on a single piece of paper that you can stick on the wall in your study area, or in the front of your study notes. It is better to use some type of diagram or mind-map rather than a list, but the most important thing is that you capture the entire syllabus for each exam on one sheet.

This one-page overview is of great psychological importance. With it, you will have captured everything you need to learn for your exam on a single piece of paper! Surely, learning the contents of just one piece of paper is manageable?

Prioritise Topics.

Having identified what you need to learn for the exam, you can now start to sort the topics into a priority for study.

You know (or should know – see next section) which topics are more important and are most likely to come up in the exam. You also know what topics you are already confident with and those where you need to put in more work. Therefore, your study plan should not be spread equally across all areas of the syllabus. Rather, you should concentrate on the key syllabus areas and those areas where you feel you are weakest.

Give these key syllabus areas more time and greater priority. In practice, this means that you should study these priority topics first. This will give you longer to spend on them and more opportunity to revisit and rework questions many times before the exam.

If you leave these key topics until the end, you will not give yourself enough time to adequately learn and consolidate your knowledge. Remember that "to revise" quite literally means "look at again". So, if you look at a topic several times over a longer period your understanding will be greater, and more will stick in your memory.

Gain A Good Understanding of The Examiner's Style and Priorities

An important aspect of setting your study priorities is gaining a good understanding of your examiner's priorities. Every examiner has their own style of writing exam questions. I have been an accounting examiner for over 20 years with several different professional bodies and academic institutions. I am therefore very aware of my own style of exam questions and of the style of other examiners.

The more you are able to understand a particular examiner's style, the easier you will be able to write good answers to their questions. I therefore consider this an essential part of exam preparation. You should review as many past exam papers as you can for the exam that you are sitting.

Here is my 6-step strategy for analysing exam papers:

1. Look at the overall structure of the exam paper. Most exam papers have the same structure at every exam session. For example, the paper may have one compulsory question worth 50 marks and then three option questions each worth 25 marks, of which two must be answered.

2. Look at the structure of individual questions. For example, a 50-mark question may be broken down into 4 parts, each dealing with a different aspect of the question scenario. Look for the pattern in these parts of a question. There is usually a clear structure to multi-part questions.

   Here is a question about reporting and accountability that focuses on the agency relationship of a company's directors. In the question scenario a company owned by the national government has been involved in a large environmental disaster which has had a negative impact on its reputation. The requirements of the question are as follows:

   Required:

   (a) Explain what an agency relationship is.

   (b) Examine the board of directors' current agency relationship and objectives.

   (c) Briefly explain how these would differ if the company had private shareholders.

(d) Draft a briefing note for the board of directors which explains how the roles and responsibilities of directors apply to the events set out in the scenario.

If you read through parts (a) to (d) of this question you can see that there is a logical sequence and structure to the whole question.

Part (a) asks you for a simple definition. This requires a straightforward explanation of material from the syllabus. But, at the same time, part (a) acts as a clear signal as to what area of the syllabus the question is examining.

Part (b) develops from part (a) by asking you to apply your knowledge to the scenario presented in the question (this scenario is not set out above, but ran to two full pages on the exam paper).

Part (c) takes you beyond the facts set out in the scenario to test your broader understanding of the topic.

Part (d) takes you into a more detailed analysis of how the syllabus applies to the scenario. You must now be able to identify specific aspects of directors' responsibilities and be able to evaluate how and whether they apply to the scenario. This requires a higher level of skill (analysis and evaluation). Furthermore, your professional writing skills are being tested, as you must write your answer in the form of a briefing note to the board.

This analysis reveals the underlying logic of the

question and how the question is structured to take you from a straightforward task (defining a concept from the syllabus) through to higher level skills of analysis and professional writing. If you are able to analyse questions in this way it will help you to better understand the structure and style of the questions you will encounter in the exams you have to sit.

3. Identify the key areas of the syllabus that the examiner regularly returns to. You can do this by creating a table of topics and plotting their frequency. Syllabus areas that are often examined are clearly the areas that the examiner feels are most important and that you need to demonstrate competence in in order to pass.

   For example, advanced level financial reporting exams tend to place a strong emphasis on your ability to construct consolidated financial statements. If you are going to pass such an exam, it is important that you ensure that you can produce consolidated financial statements as accurately as possible. Other areas of the syllabus, such as accounting for leases, for example, while still being important, may not be "core" to exam success in the same way.

4. Read the published answers for past exam papers. I will discuss how to use model answers in more detail later. At this stage, recognise the importance of reading the examiner's own answers. These are usually published with past exam papers. Not only do they provide a useful insight into what the

examiner thinks a good answer looks like, but also the examiner often adds notes and comments about what he or she expects students to write, or tips on errors to be avoided.

5. Read the examiner's reports. Most examination bodies publish an examiner's report following each exam session. This contains valuable information, as it is the examiner's evaluation of how well candidates answered questions. The examiner will discuss frequent mistakes they encountered and other ways in which candidates lost marks. You can use these reports to learn from previous candidates' mistakes and to avoid making them yourself.

6. Read technical articles written and published by the examiner. Most professional bodies encourage their examiners to write technical articles for their magazine, student magazine or website that relate to their particular exam. These articles may cover exam technique or the technical details of a specific accounting issue. You should pay close attention to these articles as not only can they supplement your other study materials, but they are also often an indication of what topics are coming up in future exam papers.

Have Study Goals and Make Them SMART

Your study plan should have goals and these should follow the SMART model. That is to say, they should be specific, measurable, achievable, relevant, and time constrained. Let's look at each of these in turn:

Specific

Don't just tell yourself "I will revise financial accounting today". You need to be specific about which particular area of your financial accounting syllabus you are going to revise. You need to ensure that you cover all the important areas of the syllabus in your study plan. In the work that you have already done in prioritising topics and understanding the examiner's priorities you should have identified that some topics will be more important than others and some topics will be larger than others. These will therefore require more time. For example, you may decide to spend 3 consecutive study periods on consolidations but only one study period on accounting for leases. You must make this decision based upon your own understanding of the syllabus and the relative importance that the examiner places on different topics.

Measurable

Break your studying down into actionable and measurable steps. Do not have open ended study sessions such as 'I will study as much as I can in the next

2 hours.'. Rather, have specific, measurable outcomes for each study session. For example: 'I will work an exam question under exam conditions and then review the model answer.' You should have a clear outcome for each study session. As well as ensuring that you cover all the work you need to, there are great psychological benefits in doing this, which I discuss below.

Achievable

Do not be unrealistic about what you can achieve in each study session. It is damaging to set yourself goals that are too demanding. You will fall behind, which will cause stress and panic. It is better to set less demanding targets that you are able to consistently meet or exceed. This will keep you in a positive frame of mind about your progress.

Relevant

Your study sessions should be results based. Spend your time on activities that will directly improve your exam performance. There is a hierarchy of activities that you should follow. Keep to the activities at the top of this list as much as possible:

1. Practicing exam questions

2. Learning models, formats and formulae

3. Reading notes

4. Reading textbooks

Why do I prioritise practice of exam questions? The answer is very simple. Writing answers to exam questions is what you need to be able to do, so that is the skill you need to practice.

Time Constrained

It is much better for your concentration if you break your studying down into short sessions. If you spend 2 hours on your studies every day you will achieve more than saving all of this up and trying to spend 14 hours in one day per week.

However you chose to timetable your study, it is important that each study session is time constrained. It is counter-productive to spend too much time revising. Your ability to learn and retain will decrease. You will become exhausted and this in turn will have a negative impact on your state of mind. It will also have a negative impact on your performance in the exam if you go into the exam in a state of exhaustion.

Create Your Study Timetable

If you have done all the preparation work I have described so far, you should now be in a position to write out a study timetable following the SMART rules.

There are four main benefits of having a written study timetable to follow:

1. A timetable gives structure and order to your exam preparation. By putting a timetable in place and then following it you will ensure that you have covered everything you need to before the exam.

2. A timetable will reduce your levels of stress. Being in the right state of mind during your exam preparation is extremely important and you should do everything you can to keep your stress levels low. One of the most important ways of doing this is feeling that you are on top of your studies. If you have a study plan and you stick to it, you can be confident that your studies are going well and you do not need to panic.

3. You have a very useful measure of whether you are actually keeping up in your studies and therefore a basis for taking action if you are not.

4. You have a clear justification for doing other things. For example, if you have timetabled 2 hours to look at a specific topic and work a couple of questions, and you answer those questions to your satisfaction, then you can finish that study session with a clear conscience. You can go and meet with friends, spend time with the family, play some sport or whatever else you would like to do, without that little voice in your head telling you that you should be studying. No, you should not be studying! You have a plan. You are working to that plan. Your studying is going

well.

Have a Clear Structure and Outcome for Each Study Session

Each of your scheduled study sessions should be structured with a beginning, middle and end:

- The beginning of each session should be a brief re-cap of what you studied in the last session.

- The middle should involve moving on to new material, focusing primarily on practising exam questions.

- The end should be a review of what you have covered in the session, noting any areas you need to spend more time on. This will provide the starting point for your next study session.

Chapter Summary

This chapter has looked at how you can lay down the foundation for a structured, thorough and systematic approach to exam preparation. Rather than just rushing into reading your notes or practicing questions, you should take time to structure your studies as suggested in this chapter. This will ensure that you used your study time most efficiently and effective. The next chapter will look in more detail at how you can increase the effectiveness of your study time.

Key Points:

- Make a study plan – now!
- Be realistic about the time you have available.
- Prioritise topics – some are more important than others
- Have clearly defined outcomes to every study session.

CHAPTER 3:
INCREASE THE EFFECTIVENESS OF YOUR STUDY TIME

This chapter is about how to study smarter rather than study harder. The key to effective exam preparation does not lie in throwing yourself into endless hours of tedious study. Rather, it lies in employing the techniques that have been proven to work.

Quality Over Quantity

There are two issues that you are trying to balance in your approach to exam preparation:

- You need to find the learning approaches and modes of study that work most effectively for you.

- You need to manage your stress levels.

A certain amount of stress is good for you. That is what drives you to switch off the television and do some studying. However, too much stress means that your study time is not as effective as it might be. If your stress levels become too high, then your effectiveness falls apart totally and your studies will grind to a halt. This is why one of the themes throughout this book is finding methods and techniques to manage your stress levels, both during exam preparation and in the exam itself.

Chunk It Down!

The key to effective and efficient studying is to break your time and effort down into short, powerful and highly focused periods. Here are some techniques to help you do this:

The Pomodoro Technique

The Pomodoro technique involves breaking your work down into sessions of 25 minutes with a short break (5 minutes) between each session. After 4 such sessions (2 hours) you should take a longer break.

The technique was developed in the 1980s by Francesco Cirillo, who used a kitchen time in the shape of a tomato to time his work sessions. Hence the name pomodoro, which refers to the tomato.

The idea is to stay fully focused on and immersed in your studying throughout this short 25-minute session. Don't allow distractions: don't check emails or Facebook; don't answer the telephone. You can do these things between sessions, or better still, after you have completed your full two-hour cycle of study.

In order to apply the Pomodoro technique, you need a place where you can study undisturbed for a 2-hour period, and a timer. You can use the timer on your mobile phone, but don't then be tempted to check your phone, or be distracted by message notifications. If this is a risk, it is better to buy a cheap timer and put your mobile away.

Take Regular Breaks

It is not a good idea to attempt a marathon study session that lasts all day (or worse, all night). There are studies that have shown that you best retain what you do in the first and the last few minutes of a study session. A lot of what happens in the middle of a long block of study is easily forgotten. You will therefore be much more effective by breaking your study up into short sessions with regular breaks.

Here is an example of how you can use this technique to structure a two-hour study session to maximise your learning potential. Let's say that the aim of your study session is to successfully work through two 30-minute exam questions:

- Put your timer on for 30 minutes and attempt the first question under exam conditions.

- When the timer goes off, take a 5-minute break. Get up and move around during this break. Do some stretching. Your eyes have been focused at a short distance for 30 minutes, so look out of the window or across the room to let your eyes relax and work at a different distance. You may like to get yourself a drink to take back to your study area.

- Work through the model answer to see how well you have done. If necessary, rework parts of computations. If there are points made in the model answer to a written question that you did not cover in your own answer, then add these to your notes. You may want to look up the topic in your notes or textbook. You can give yourself 20 minutes to do this.

- Give yourself another short break for 5 minutes. This will take your study time to 60 minutes, half of your allotted study session.

- Repeat the cycle with the second question. (A further 60 minutes).

- Once you have completed the cycle for the second question, finish this study session and do something else. You need to take a longer break after two hours of study.

Use Spaced Repetition

Repetition is the mother of learning. This is so important I will say it again: repetition is the mother of learning. It is therefore essential that you regularly go back over what you have been studying and review it again. To 'revise' literally means to 'look at again'. Revision is about looking at the things you need to learn again and again and again.

There has been a lot of research about how to best do this. The consensus is that the most effective approach is one known as spaced repetition. Using this technique, you revisit the material you are trying to learn at regular but increasing intervals.

For example, here is a typical spaced repetition schedule for lodging something in your long-term memory:

1. First revision

2. Revise again – next day

3. Revise again – After 2 days

4. Revise again – After 1 weeks

5. Revise again after 2 weeks

Build this spaced repetition approach into your study timetable.

Over Learn Your Exam Topics

Over learning means continuing to practice something after you can already do it. Musicians and athletes do this all the time. A concert violinist learning a new a tune does not stop practicing the first time she plays it correctly! She keeps practicing it over and over, even when she can play it perfectly.

Apply the same principle to your exam preparation. The exam will be a 'performance' in which you will have to accomplish tasks such as preparing a tax computation or compiling a set of financial statements. You should practice these performance skills, even after you can do them well. Hone them, polish them, refine them.

You should aim be to be so familiar with the format and process of preparing a tax computation that you barely need to think about it. Then, when faced with such a question in the exam, you can concentrate your mental energy on the specific facts and details of the question, rather than on the basic mechanics of putting the computation together.

Don't Over Study

Over learning is not the same as over studying. Over learning, as explained above, is continuing to practice a skill after you have learned it. Over studying is simply doing too much studying. Over learning is good. Over studying is bad. Fight the urge to over study.

As you approach the date of your exams there will be a little voice in your head telling you that you need to do more studying. The temptation will always be to try and do more. More is better, right? Not necessarily so. Obviously, doing too little studying will not help you. You need to do enough to be adequately prepared for the exam. However, over studying can be counterproductive. It will wear you down. Your enthusiasm and interest for your studies may well dwindle, and you will become tired. Beyond a certain point, your effectiveness will fall off dramatically and more studying could actually be damaging. It is therefore better to restrict yourself to fewer and shorter study sessions, all of which are productive, rather than to try and spend hour after hour slogging away.

So how much is too much? It all depends on your situation and how many other demands you have on your time and energy. If you are trying to revise alongside working full-time and looking after a family, then you will have much less time and energy available to dedicate to your studying than if you are a full-time student.

Reward Yourself for Achievement

By now you should have made yourself a written study plan in which you have clearly timetabled slots of time for your studies. You know exactly what you will be doing in each study session. You have a clear outcome to each study session. You should now be working to that study plan and sticking to it.

If you are doing this then you can reward yourself for your achievement. Give yourself breaks and treats. You should not be studying for 14 hours a day. You should be out doing other things that refresh your body and refresh your brain and therefore mean that you will be more effective in your learning and retention.

I recommend that you include in your timetable other activities that give you this opportunity to refresh yourself. These should be things you enjoy doing and preferably things that are healthy and good for you both mentally and physically.

Try to get regular exercise. Even if this is just a short 15 to 20 minute walk every day.

It is essential that you make time for things that you enjoy. Meet with friends, listen to music, read a novel. You must balance your study time with activities that will refresh you, if you are going to achieve peak performance in your exam preparation.

Chapter Summary

Effective study is about learning and retaining the most material in the shortest time, with the least effort. There are well established techniques for doing this. So, get smart and employ these techniques to your own study. Become highly effective in your studying. We will further explore how to be more effective in the next chapter, in which we look at different modes of learning and how you can employ those that work best for you.

Key Points:

- Chunk your study time down into short sessions with regular breaks

- Use the Pomodoro technique of timed 25 minute, highly focused study sessions.

- Take regular breaks during longer study sessions.

- Use spaced repetition to learn and retain important material

- Over learn, but don't over study

- Reward your achievements.

CHAPTER 4:
EXPLORING MODES OF LEARNING

I hope that you have realised by this point that the chapters which make up Part 1 of this book are a quest to maximise the effectiveness of your exam preparation. We have looked at how you can create the space for your studying, how to best structure the use of that space, and the techniques which ensure you use it most efficiently and effectively.

In this chapter we will look at different modes of learning and how a good understanding of these modes will help you study in a way that works best for you.

The Importance of Active Learning

I cannot emphasise too strongly the importance of engaging in active learning as opposed to passive learning. Too many students believe that revision should be focused around simply reading through their notes or reading the textbook. This is passive learning.

In the exam you will have to write answers to questions. You therefore need to practice this activity to prepare for the exam. If you had a swimming test coming up which required you to swim 1,000 metres, would you just sit at the side of the pool reading a book about how to swim? I certainly hope not! Of course, you would get in the water and practice swimming.

In a similar vein, if taking an accounting exam involves writing a business report, preparing accounts, or doing a tax computation, then these are the skills you need to practice. In the exam you will have to write answers to exam questions. You therefore need to practice writing answers to exam questions. This means actually writing answers. It does not mean reading the question and then reading the model answer and telling yourself "oh yes, that is the answer I would have written".

Therefore, the primary focus of your exam preparation should be question practice. However, there are other activities you can include in your study schedule. This is an opportunity to mix it up and have more fun, making your study time more interesting, more enjoyable and therefore more effective.

Explore Learning Styles

We are not all the same and we learn differently. Some people are visual learners, others are auditory learners. Some people really enjoy reading, others hate it. Some people are introverts who love studying alone, whereas others are extroverts who prefer to be with others if possible. Some people have great self-discipline and have no problem in studying for 2 hours without distraction, whereas others will be distracted by the smallest thing.

One of the most interesting and fun things about exploring different learning styles is finding how you can engage your different senses as part of your learning experience. Think of ways you can engage your sense of hearing, sight, speaking, touch (and if you can manage it, smell). Studies have shown that the more senses you engage, the more you are able to remember.

Sound can be an important factor in memory. Have you ever heard a song on the radio that has immediately brought back memories of what you were doing when you first heard it? Music is very powerful. Listening to music whilst studying can increase concentration. There have been some studies which suggest that concentration, learning and memory can be enhanced by listening to classical baroque music whilst you study.

You can engage your auditory senses in many ways. You could, for example, listen to recordings that are relevant to the topics you are learning. These may be recordings of classes or lectures that you have attended. They may be podcasts or recordings from YouTube.

You can also create your own recordings if you have a suitable recording device such as a mobile phone. You could even ask a friend who is studying for the same exam to make some recordings and you could exchange recordings with them. Having recordings that you can listen to whilst travelling, going for a walk, or exercising in the gym is a great way of engaging different senses as part of your learning process and of finding ways to extend your learning and revision beyond your formal revision sessions.

Focused vs Diffuse Thinking

Your brain uses two different modes to process information. These modes are known as focused and diffuse thinking.

Focused thinking is the mode we usually regard as 'thinking'. It involves concentrating on the matter at hand. This type of thinking uses the brain's prefrontal cortex. It requires a high level of attention. When we do this, we concentrate explicitly on a problem and exclude any extraneous information. In order to apply focused thinking, we need to remove all distractions from the matter at hand. This is the type of thinking we engage when practicing exam questions, reading notes and learning formats and formulae.

Diffuse thinking, on the other hand, is not highly focused. It involves taking a step back from the immediate problem and looking at the bigger picture. It is a thinking process that can go on in the background, whilst we are doing other things. It works effectively if we let our mind wander or be distracted by something else. The conscious, focused mind is relaxed. You might call this processing time. It is important to give your brain time for this type of thinking to supplement and compliment the highly focused thinking involved in question practice and reading. Go for a walk or for a run; go to the gym; wash the dishes. These all activities that will give your brain space for some diffuse thinking.

The Feynman Technique

This technique is named after the Nobel-Prize physicist Richard Feynman. Feynman suggested that if you want to understand something you should explain it to someone else. Teaching both tests and reinforces your own learning and aids your understanding. It helps you understand the principles of what you are studying, rather than just learning them by rote. When you try to explain something you very quickly find out whether or not your own understanding is solid. (Having spent many years as an accounting tutor I know this from first-hand experience) By trying to explain something to someone else you can identify where your understanding is shaky and needs more work.

I strongly encourage you to aspire to this deeper level of learning and understanding. The better you understand the principles of the material you are learning, the more able you will be to deal with new and complex exam questions.

For example, how well do you understand the principles of the payback period method of investment appraisal? Can you explain:

1. What is the payback period?

2. What does it tell us about the returns from an investment?

3. What does it tell us about the risks of an investment?

4. What does it NOT tell us that we need to know?

5. What are the computational limitations of the

technique?

If you are able to explain answers to each of these questions, then you have a pretty good understanding of the principles of payback period analysis. If you cannot explain them, in simple, clear language, then perhaps you need to improve your understanding.

Here is a method for applying the Feynman technique in four simple steps:

1. Pick the topic you want to learn and write it down

2. Explain the topic in as simple language as possible. Include examples in your explanation. You can write out your explanation, or you can speak it out loud. If you have a willing friend or family member, they can be your audience. If you are studying with a friend (see section below on finding a 'study-buddy') you can take it in turns to be teacher and student.

3. Identify areas of your explanation that were shaky, or issues that you were not able to explain. Go back to your notes or study books to improve your understanding of these areas. Google the topic. Look for YouTube videos on the topic. Make more notes.

4. Identify where you have not been able to explain in simple language. Have you used complex terminology or formulae? Can you explain these in a clearer, simpler way? A useful technique is to constantly ask 'why?' like a small child does. 'Why is this the case?'; 'Why does that formula work?'

Find a Study-Buddy

If you struggle to find the self-discipline to stick to your study plan, then you may benefit from finding yourself a study-buddy. Even if you do not have such a problem, working with a study-buddy is a great way of making your study sessions more fun.

It is better to find someone who is also studying for an exam. It helps if they are studying for the same exam as you, but it is not totally necessary. The idea is to find somebody who will give you mutual support in your efforts. There are a number of ways that you can do this.

You can make a study-buddy "date". This involves agreeing a time and place where you will meet in order to study together. The advantage of this is that you are committing not just yourself but to someone else. If you fail to turn up, you are letting down yourself and your study-buddy. There is therefore more psychological pressure to keep that date.

There will also be psychological pressure to get some work done during that study date, provided you both agree not to act as a distraction to each other! For example, if you both agree to work an exam question for 30 minutes you can act as each other's invigilator. You can make sure that the other person does not start checking their phone after 10 minutes, or just give up because they find the question difficult. Of course, this will not work if you both give up and just start chatting. There has to be total commitment from both partners for this study-buddy system to work.

The study-buddy system also gives you the

opportunity to practice the Feynman technique that I discussed above. You can, for example, give your study-buddy 10 minutes to explain a theory or model as if they were teaching you. After the 10 minutes you can swap, and you explain something to your study-buddy for a further 10 minutes.

Another fun way to work with a study-buddy is to quiz each other on topics. You can alternatively fire questions at each other and challenge each other to remember key models, formulae or acronyms.

Even if you cannot find someone else who is studying for the same exam as you, it may be possible to find a friend or family member who is able to engage in some of these activities with you to support your studying. They do not necessarily need to understand the topic you are revising. For example, you could create some flashcards with questions on one side and answers on the other and get your study-buddy to question you using these flashcards.

The most important thing about using a study-buddy is that it makes the study process less lonely. Spending hours alone, hunched over a desk, practising questions can be a very lonely experience. Although question practice is essential preparation for your exam, you can mix it up with some of the activities I have suggested above in order to create variety and interest in your study schedule.

Chapter Summary

In this chapter you have seen that there is more than one approach to successful exam preparation. Active learning is important, and many students fail to recognise this, wasting too much time on passive learning strategies. At the same time, there are many ways to mix up you studying to keep it fresh and interesting and to make it less of a lonely experience.

Key Points:

- Prioritize active learning over passive learning.

- Make your studies fun. Fun = more engagement = better learning and retention.

- Mix it up – engage in a range of different approaches to learning to provide variety and interest.

- Work with others – your exam preparation does not have to be a lonely odyssey.

CHAPTER 5:
IMPROVE THE EFFECTIVENESS OF YOUR READING

Students frequently complain to me that they struggle to fit in all the reading they need to do. Many complain that they have read a textbook but cannot remember what they read. When I quiz them on these problems what usually comes to light is the fact that they do not know how to approach reading a textbook in an effective manner.

Therefore, in this chapter I will share with you the techniques that underpin good academic reading skills.

Don't Read A Textbook Like A Novel

I hope this point is obvious to you. You read a novel by starting at the beginning and reading it through, page by page, to the end. This is because a novel is telling a story, with a plot that unfolds as you read. To enjoy the novel, you need to read through it sequentially and follow the twists and turns of the plot.

A textbook, on the other hand, is not telling a story. It is imparting knowledge. You are reading it simply to learn and understand the material you need for your exams. You should therefore adopt a very different reading strategy – one that enables you to learn what you need as quickly and efficiently as possible.

Here is a simple five step strategy for reading a textbook:

1. **Get the big picture first.**

    Get an overview of what the book is about and what it contains by firstly reading the back cover and then looking through the contents page. Then have a flick through the book.

2. **Identify which chapters you want to read and in what order.**

    You may not need to read the whole book. You may feel that you already have a good understanding of some subjects but need to do more detailed reading on others. You may be reading the book to learn more about just one specific topic.

3. **Read for the big ideas**

    Turn to a chapter that you want to read. Flick through the chapter to get a feel of how long it is. How many pages does the chapter contain? How much material does it cover? What are the main or 'big' ideas of the chapter? How many of these are there? (for example, a chapter on investment appraisal may have 4 'big ideas', being the 4 main traditional investment appraisal techniques). Get a feel for how long you need to spend on the chapter.

4. **Read for the key points**

    If there is a chapter summary at the end of the chapter, or a 'key points' section, read this first. Then read the chapter introduction. Look at the main headings and sub-headings. Look at the diagrams, charts and pictures.

5. Read the detail

Finally, read the detail of those sections you identify as important. Underline, highlight and take notes as you do so. Good notes are important. Chapter 6 of this book looks in more detail at effective notetaking.

The Importance of Understanding Principles

Rote learning of material may work for you for basic level exams in some subjects. However, when it comes to more advanced level accounting exams this is simply not enough. You need to develop an understanding of the principles that underpin the models and theories that you are learning. Only by doing this will you develop the analytical, critical and evaluation skills necessary to answer the types of unknown and highly specific scenarios you will find in advanced level accounting exams.

For example, if studying investment appraisal, you can rote learn the traditional evaluation techniques and how to apply them. But you should aim to go deeper than this. What exactly does one need to analyse and evaluate when making an investment decision? What are the key factors? And importantly, how are these addressed by the different investment appraisal techniques?

Imagine you are answering an exam question that asks you to calculate the payback period of two different investment opportunities and to comment on which one is the most favourable.

You calculate that Investment A has a two-year payback period and Investment B has a four-year payback period. You therefore recommend Investment A, because you have learnt that you should choose the investment with the shorter payback period.

But why is this the case? What is it about a shorter payback period that is more attractive? And importantly, what does the payback period NOT tell us about an investment that may be equally or even more important?

The Importance of Reading Widely

The more widely you read around a subject the more you will deepen your understanding of that subject. Also, the more widely you read, the more examples, applications of models and techniques you will be exposed to. This will better prepare you to deal with new scenarios and applications of techniques that you will encounter in exam questions.

You should apply what I call 'triangulation of learning'. By this I mean that if you simply attend lectures, then you only have one point of reference for your learning. If you attend lectures and read a textbook, then you have two points of reference and double your chances of understanding the subject. If you also read other textbooks, technical articles and webpages, and watch YouTube videos, you create multiple points of reference and multiple opportunities to deepen your understanding.

Different tutors explain things differently. I have my own particular way of teaching technical subjects. Other lecturers and other authors have different ways of presenting the same material. If you expose yourself to as many different versions of explanation as you can, you will find that you pick up something new from every fresh source you turn to. Your knowledge and understanding will become more substantial and this will better equip you when it comes to the exam.

For example, your main textbook may suggest a particular approach to laying out a calculation for profit on disposal of a non-current asset. You may follow this approach, but struggle with it. If you look at two or three other textbooks, you may find a different approach which works better for you. For all of us, it usually just takes one spark of inspiration to suddenly grasp a concept that we have been struggling with. You should therefore expose yourself to as many opportunities to find these sparks as you can. With the material that is available on the Internet these days, this is not difficult to do.

Chapter Summary

Reading is an essential part of studying for accounting exams. Even if you are fortunate enough to attend regular classes, you will still need to read to deepen and broaden your knowledge and understanding. Therefore, develop a habit of reading widely, reading often, and reading effectively.

Key Points:

- Develop a good technique and a clear strategy for reading textbooks quickly and efficiently.

- Focus on understanding principles rather than just rote learning of rules, formulae or procedures.

- Read widely to broaden your knowledge and deepen your understanding.

CHAPTER 6:
PRODUCING EFFECTIVE NOTES

I can still recall being a young accounting student sitting in classes at university. We had a law lecturer who would majestically sweep into the lecture theatre and deliver an hour's lecture with no visuals (those were the days before PowerPoint), and no handouts.

I would sit through his lectures frantically trying to write down every pearl of wisdom that came from his mouth. I literally tried to transcribe the whole lecture. After several weeks of finger cramps and reams of illegible scribble, I realised that I needed to change my approach. I remember going for a coffee after one particularly frustrating lecture and asking myself "what exactly do I need to write down?". I then asked myself the more fundamental question of "Why am I actually taking notes?" I soon came to realise that what I needed to produce was a set of notes that would help me to learn and remember the key points I needed to pass the exam.

Based upon my own experiences as a student I have developed the following maxim:

Attend a class once; read a textbook once; but write, read and add to your notes multiple times.

The Art of Good Note Taking

The art of good note taking involves capturing the key

information first time, so that you never need to go back to the original source material.

Good note taking is not easy, and most of us are not good at it. But if you consciously work on improving your note taking you will save yourself a lot of time and effort. And that is what this book is about – becoming more effective and more efficient in your studies.

So, what constitutes good note taking? There is no one approach that works perfectly for everyone. There are whole books that focus specifically on note taking, so in this chapter I will simply distil the most important points (which, after all, is the essence of good note taking!)

Not Too Many Notes

Here are the two most important lessons I have learned from exploring the art of good note taking:

1. You need to produce a set of notes. Arriving at a good set of notes is a process, and not necessarily a one-off task. That production process must go beyond simply writing things down during a lecture or whilst reading a textbook. Ideas must be re-organised, re-categorised and added to as your learning and understanding develops. Material may need to be re-presented in a format and structure that is more useful to you. This will not necessarily be the format in which the notes were initially captured.

2. What you should aim to capture are the key points

– not every word, or even every idea. These key points can act as a trigger to remembering the details that you have not included in your notes.

Only Note the Most Important Things.

From my initial revelation over a post-lecture coffee as an undergraduate student, and after much further experimentation and refinement, I came up with a system of notes that work for me. This is the basis of what I have subsequently taught to many students.

This system does not involve just one style of notes, but rather involves a mixture of mind-maps, linear notes, diagrams and other formats.

Here is an example of the notes I would produce for a financial accounting exam:

1.   A one-page mind-map of the entire syllabus. The aim here is to capture the whole syllabus on just one page. In order to achieve this, you will inevitably have to be brief, but the aim is an overview, not full detail.

2.   Between four and six supporting mind-maps that explore key syllabus areas in more detail. This is your opportunity to fill in some of the details that are missing from the one-page overview.

3.   Two to three pages setting out key definitions, models, formulae, rules and principles.

4.   One separate page for each financial statement you

need to know for the exam, setting out formats with all headings.

This would result in a set of notes of approximately 15 pages for this one exam. That is a very manageable level of material.

For exams that require longer written answers, I would also add to my notes with more pages that focus on key points and arguments for me to use in my written answers. I explain this in more detail in the following section.

Mind-Mapping

In this chapter (and throughout this whole book) I refer frequently to the technique of mind-mapping. Mind-mapping is a way of presenting ideas and concepts graphically, rather than in traditional linear notes.

Mind-mapping has several advantages over linear note taking. Specifically, you can explore links between concepts, investigate their relationships, expand on ideas and generate new ideas. The graphical layout makes things easier to remember than linear notes (in fact you can use specific 'shapes' to help you remember specific mind-maps), and mind-maps are very quick and easy to produce and reproduce. You can easily add to them or change them as your understanding of a topic develops.

A detailed explanation of how to mind-map is beyond the scope of this book. However, if you are not familiar with the technique, I strongly urge you to invest some time in learning it. There are many useful resources for learning mind-mapping on the internet, and many excellent tutorial videos on YouTube.

Working with Your Notes

Your notes are not something you just create whilst reading or during classes. They should be at the core of your learning and exam preparation. Your notes are a vehicle for capturing your understanding of topics, and then developing, deepening, refining and exploring that understanding.

One of the big advantages of concise, non-linear notes, such as mind-maps is that they are easy to update, refine and reorganise. This means that you can constantly develop and improve your notes. The activity of re-drawing mind maps or reorganising them is also an important part of the learning process. By re-drawing your mind maps you are exploring the material and reinforcing your understanding.

Here is an example of how you might work with a mind-map that sets out your understanding of internal controls for an audit exam:

(a) You attend a lecture on internal controls and make notes during the lecture.

(b) After the lecture you review your notes and, exploring your understanding, arrange them into a mind-map.

(c) You read your textbook and learn more about the topic. You add this new knowledge to your mind-map.

(d) You attempt a past exam question on internal controls. You then review the examiner's suggested solution and find new points you had not previously learned. You add these new points to your mind-map.

(e) You redraw your original mind-map to better integrate the new points you learned from reading the textbook and past question answers.

(f) As part of your revision, you give yourself 5 minutes to fully reproduce your mind-map without referring to the original. You then compare this to the original and fill in any parts you missed.

I hope that you can see that this is an iterative process that should continue throughout your studies and your revision. Your notes are not static but should be constantly evolving to capture your deepening understanding.

Chapter Summary

Good note taking is key to effective studying. Invest time in your note taking skills and invest time in your notes. Work with your notes constantly throughout your studies and make them your best friend.

Key Points:

- Consciously work on your note-taking skills and constantly try to improve your notes.

- Treat your notes as your first reference point for revision.

- Keep your notes simple and brief, capturing the key points you need as succinctly as possible.

- Updating, refining and reorganising your notes should be an integral part of your study activities.

CHAPTER 7:
PREPARING FOR NUMERICAL QUESTIONS

Most accounting exams involve some element of number crunching. That is just the nature of the discipline. Financial accounting, management accounting, taxation and financial management exams, in particular, tend to be built upon your ability to deal with numbers.

It is therefore important that you adequately prepare yourself for the different types of numerical question you might encounter, and that you develop a strategy for answering such questions. We will look more closely at exam strategy in Part 2 of this book. For now, let's look at how you can best prepare yourself before the exam.

Learn Formats

You should learn the layout of financial statements and other important formats by heart. Your study notes should include the format and layout of each statement you might need to produce in the exam.

Practice writing these formats out in full at least once per week, without copying from your notes. It is important that you continue to do this, even after you get the formats correct. This is a process called 'over learning'. It is what musicians and athletes do (see chapter 3). You should do the same with your practice of financial statement formats. It is important that you know all these formats and can quickly produce them in the exam without having to think about it. You can then concentrate your time and energy in the exam on filling in the correct numbers within the structure of the format. You do not want to be wasting precious time during the exam trying to remember the sequence of headings in a financial statement. You need to be able to concentrate on inserting the correct numbers.

You can produce your own list of formats that you need to learn, depending upon the subject matter of your exam. Here is an example of the formats you may need to learn for a financial reporting exam:

- Balance sheet (Statement of Financial Position)
- Income statement
- Cash flow statement
- Statement of Retained earnings

Depending upon the syllabus of your exam, you may also need to learn other formats such as those found in the notes to financial statements.

An important aspect of learning formats is understanding the principles that underpin them. If you understand the principles, then you will be able to remember the formats more easily and you will be to apply them far more intelligently.

An example of this is the order in which current

assets appear on a balance sheet. Here is a typical list of current assets in the order they appear:

- Inventories
- Trade and other receivables
- Derivative financial assets
- Current tax assets
- Short-term investments
- Cash and cash equivalents

Do you notice that each category of asset increases in liquidity as you work your way down the list? Cash and cash equivalents are the most liquid assets, as liquidity is (by definition) about access to cash. On the other hand, inventories are the least liquid current asset because they must first be sold (converted to receivables) and then the receivables collected before they are translated into cash. Inventory is therefore two steps away from cash. So, an easy way to help you remember the sequence in which to list current assets is to refer to their relative liquidity.

Learn Procedures

You will find that for most accounting computations there is a clear and systematic approach that you can take. If you are learning in college, then hopefully your tutor will teach you a systematic approach to each type of computational question. If you are self-studying, then you should refer to the textbooks you have available or to other online resources and be sure to make a note of the steps involved in the most common types of computation that you will face.

Here is an example to illustrate what I mean. When preparing a balance sheet and income statement from a trial balance, you can follow these 4 steps:

Step 1: Write out all the key headings for both the income statement and the balance sheet. You should give yourself plenty of space to do this. Start each statement on a separate page and ensure that you leave sufficient gaps to be able to later add any headings or subheadings that you may have overlooked.

Step 2: For those numbers that you can transfer straight from the trial balance onto the financial statements, do so now. Remember, that if the trial balance balances, then your accounts will only balance if you transfer each number once and enter it correctly - debits as either an asset or an expense: credits as either a liability or income. For those figures that you know are going to require adjustment, for example accruals, prepayments, bad or doubtful debts, depreciation or amortisation, enter the number onto your answer page but as a note in the margin or underneath your heading, so that you can add the adjustment and show your workings directly on the page.

Step 3: Now make your accounting adjustments. Remember that, because you are adjusting the trial balance which already balances, each adjustment you make must be entered twice: once as a debit and once as a credit. A good rule of thumb (although unfortunately it does not apply 100% of the time) is that when making accounting adjustments one entry will be in the income statement and the other entry will be in the balance sheet. Remember, a debit must be entered either as an asset or an expense; a credit must be entered either as a liability or income.

Step 4: By this point you should have entered all the figures on to your financial statements. Where you have transferred these into workings such as depreciation or bad debts, you should now complete those workings and enter the resultant figure into the correct space in your financial statements. You can then add up the financial statements. Start with the income statement and work your way down, calculating gross profit, EBIT etc. Transfer the figure you arrive at for retained profit onto your balance sheet and then add up the balance sheet. If you have transferred each figure from the trial balance to only one place in the financial statements, and have entered each financial adjustment twice, then your balance sheet should balance. If it does not, have a quick look through your figures and workings to see if you can identify a mistake. If you cannot find where you have made the mistake, then don't worry. Even with a balance sheet that does not balance, you will have picked up a substantial proportion of the marks for the figures that you have entered correctly.

I hope you can see from this example that preparing yourself for a question like this in the exam (and this is a very common style of question) involves 2 stages:

1. Learn the formats and headings of the financial statements

2. Learn and practice the 4-step procedure set out above.

You should apply this principle to all other areas of your study to create a systematic approach to answering numeric questions that you have prepared and practiced before the exam.

Understand Formulae

The best way to remember formulae is to understand them. With every formula that you are trying to learn, try to understand what that formula is doing.

I find that many students struggle to remember the formulae for the ratios they need for financial analysis. When I challenge them to explain to me what the ratio means, that is to say, what the ratio tells us about the business, then they are much more able to remember the formula.

An illustration of this is the financial ratio Return on Capital Employed (ROCE). This is one of the easiest formulae to remember because the formula is in the name! The formula for ROCE is return (financial return, i.e. profit) on (that is to say on top of, or divided by) capital employed (the money that is invested in the business in order to earn that return). Mathematically this formula gives you a fraction that you can express as a percentage by multiplying it by 100%.

What about a more complex formula such as Inventory Turnover Period? Firstly, you need to establish what the ratio is telling us about a business. If you look in a textbook on financial analysis, you will see that this ratio is classified as an 'efficiency' ratio: It is a measure of how efficiently short-term resources (inventory) are being used. In what way does this ratio tell us about efficient asset usage? To understand this, I suggest that you ask yourself a series of questions:

1. What does the ratio literally mean?

The cost of sales (in the income statement) represents the cost of all inventory sold throughout the year. If we divide the inventory held (in the statement of financial position) by the cost of sales, we find what fraction of the year's inventory requirement is currently being held. To express this as a time period we can multiply it by 365 to give the number of days (because there are 365 days in a year). If you have an inventory turnover period of 30 days, this means that the business is holding 30 days of inventory.

2. What does a change in the ratio mean?

If sales remained constant, but the Inventory Turnover Period fell from 30 days to 20 days, this means that the business can generate the same level of sales with less inventory. It is therefore using its resources (inventory) more efficiently: Less money tied up in inventory is generating the same level of sales. On the other hand, if the ratio increased to 40 days, the business requires more inventory to generate its sales and is therefore using that resource less efficiently.

3. What does a comparison with another business mean?

If you had 2 otherwise identical businesses, but one had an Inventory Turnover Period of 20 days and the other 40 days, which is the better? In terms of efficiency, we would have to say that the business with the shorter Inventory Turnover Period is better, as it is generating the same level of sales with less cash tied up in inventory. i.e., it is more efficient.

4. What factors are at play here?

By asking this question you are trying to broaden your understanding of the ratio from the immediate mathematics of the formula to a wider business context.

A business holds inventory in order to be able to meet customer demand. But inventory ties up cash that could be used elsewhere in the business. It therefore has a cost. There is both a real cost in terms of storage space and potential loss through damage, theft or obsolescence, and an opportunity cost, for example, in not using the cash to repay loans and reduce interest charges.

Holding too much inventory is therefore not an

efficient use of working capital. However, holding too little inventory may result in stock-outs, with disruption to production, missed sales, lost customers and a negative impact on business reputation. Therefore, an inventory holding period that is too long is not good, but one that is too short may also not be good. This is a real-world business problem faced by many businesses every day. It is a problem that some businesses have sought to overcome through the introduction of systems such as Just-In-Time inventory management. This involves eliminating inventory entirely and co-ordinating supply chains to ensure that resources are in place exactly when needed.

Armed with the understanding that this question and answer process generates, it is much easier not only to remember the formula for the Inventory Turnover Period, but also to make more intelligent and business-relevant comments when interpreting the ratio in an exam question.

Furthermore, when you understand that both the Trade Receivables Collection Period and the Trade Payables Payment Period are calculated following exactly the same principles as the Inventory Turnover Period, it becomes much easier to remember all three formulae in the same way.

The above are examples for understanding and remembering just a few of the formulae for financial ratios. Once you understand the principles of what you are doing you can extend this to remembering more complex formulae in other areas of your studies such as

IRR, WACC and CAPM.

I hope that my examples above convince you of the worth of moving away from a rote-learning approach to one that seeks a deeper understanding of the formulae you are studying. If you do so:

- You will remember the formulae with greater ease

- You will be able to discuss the results of your calculations in greater detail

- You will develop better business sense

- You will find the learning process more interesting and rewarding, which in turn aids learning and memory.

The Feynman technique that I explained in Chapter 4 can help you in this process.

Practicing Exam Questions

My advice above on learning formats, procedures and formulae is about laying the foundation to be able to attempt exam questions. Once this foundation is laid you must build upon it by practising proper exam questions.

Always practice exam questions under timed conditions and attempt to answer as much as you can in the time available. Once you have done as much as you can, and only then, turn to the model answer and compare your answer to this. If you have made mistakes, highlight them in your answer and write out the correct procedure or numbers from the model answer.

If you got most of the question right, then perhaps you can put this question aside and move on to practice others. However, if you are not happy with your answer, then keep the question and come back to it at a later study session. Attempt the question again and see if you get more of the answer right this next time. Do not be afraid of repetition. There is great value in repeatedly practising the same questions. You become more familiar with the formulae, formats and techniques and therefore need to think less about these and can instead concentrate more on the specific details of the question.

What if you simply cannot answer the question? Firstly, don't panic! You will come up against this with some questions, particularly in more advanced papers. If you really have no idea about how to answer the question, then turn to the model answer. Read through the model answer, do you understand it now? If so, put the model answer aside and attempt the question without referring to it. If you still cannot answer the question, then refer to the model answer again and if necessary, simply copy out the model answer. Yes, I really did say that! By copying out the model answer you are physically going through the process of producing the answer.

It is important that you actually write out the answer. Don't just read it. This should help both your understanding and your memory. If you are still struggling to understand how the model answer is arrived at, then maybe you need to go back to your notes or even turn to a textbook or an internet resource where you can read explanations about the techniques and work through other examples.

Please note that my suggestion that you refer to a textbook come right at the end of my list of suggestions of the way that you should prepare for the exam. You should focus your exam preparation around practising questions. If you attempt a question and can answer it, or you can answer it after referring to the model answer, then there is no need for you to go back to your notes or textbook. To do so would simply be a waste of your study time. It is much better to use that time practising more questions.

Chapter Summary

In this chapter I have set out my recommended strategy for preparing for numerical questions. This strategy is built upon four activities:

1. Learn formats, formulae and calculation layouts

2. Learn the steps and procedures for each type of numerical question

3. Ensure that you understand formulae – this makes them easier to remember and easier to apply

4. Practice each type of question.

Key Points:

*   List the important formats you need to learn. Write each one out on a separate piece of paper and keep them in your revision notes. Try to reproduce the formats at least once per week without reference to your notes.

*   Learn the steps and procedures for important calculations and have a systematic approach.

*   Base your revision around exam question practice. Practice as many questions as you can, and always under timed, exam conditions

*   Only refer to your notes or your textbook if you are struggling to answer a question or to understand how the question should be answered.

CHAPTER 8:
PREPARING FOR WRITTEN QUESTIONS

I have been marking accounting exam papers for over 20 years. During this time, I have found that the main reason candidates score low marks in written questions is that they simply do not write enough. This is particularly the case in exams such as taxation, management accounting or financial management. Candidates see these exams as being mainly computational, so they focus all their time and energy on the numerical aspect of the questions. They then either ignore written questions or write short and insufficient answers.

The reality is that just about every advanced level accounting exam has a high written content. This means that you must go into the exam being prepared to write and you must know how much you need to write in order to pick up marks.

There are two sets of skills you need to develop to maximise the marks you score in written questions:

1. You must be able to generate sufficient relevant ideas to write about.

2. You must be able to prioritise your points and structure your ideas into a well-balanced answer of the appropriate length.

Be aware that these are two separate set of skills. You can generate lots of ideas, but if you simply scribble them down on your answer script without fully crafting and developing those ideas, you will not pick up enough marks. On the other hand, you can write an extremely coherent and professionally presented answer, but if it lacks substance or detail you will not pick up many marks. You therefore need to work on both skills.

A Systematic Approach to Answering Written Questions

Accepting that you need to develop two skills to answer written questions well: generate good points; and structure your points into a well-crafted answer, let's look at a systematic approach that will help you do this. Here is a four-step approach to answering written questions that I teach my accounting students.

1. Identify the models, theories or idea that are relevant to the question.

Sometimes it may be necessary to refer to a theoretical model explicitly in your answer, as is the case in the question below:

Required:

Use Porter's Diamond to explain the success of the oil industry in Zeeland.

However, the wording of some questions does not

explicitly refer to any specific model. For example:

Required:

Identify and discuss the factors that have led to ABC Inc. becoming the dominant business in the oil industry in Zeeland.

This question does not require you to use any particular model. However, you could still explicitly use Porter's Diamond to structure your answer. Alternatively, you could also answer the question without explicitly referring to any model, but simply using suitable models to help you generate ideas and to structure your points. In this case you could perhaps use both Porter's Diamond and Porter's Five Forces Model.

Whichever of these approaches you chose, don't slavishly follow a model if it is not all relevant to the context of the question. The examiner will be looking for your ability to demonstrate good understanding of what is relevant and what is not relevant to a specific scenario. A practical application of theories and models involves the ability to differentiate the relevant from the irrelevant.

For example, if you are applying Porter's Five Forces Model to a scenario in which there is no direct substitute for the goods or services in question, then that aspect of Porter's model is not relevant to the scenario and you should acknowledge this, rather than trying to force the scenario to fit the model.

In order to generate ideas quickly, I advocate the use of mind-maps (see chapter 6). Mind-maps enable you to capture ideas quickly, to explore the links between ideas and to develop lines of thought.

2. Identify real-world examples or practical experience that you can bring into your answer.

Sometimes it can be useful to draw parallels between the scenario in an exam question and a well-known real-world business situation. Don't discuss details relating to your own clients that the examiner will not know about, but you can refer to well-known international businesses or business events.

Examiners often draw their inspiration for exam questions from recent real-world events, so it is a good idea to keep yourself well-informed about what is happening in the business world. Some aspect of a recent major business event may well find its way into your exam. If you are familiar with the real event and have read about it, including the related business analysis found in newspapers and professional journals, you will be able to bring this extra insight into your exam answer.

3. Develop a well-balanced argument.

When generating your ideas for your answer, don't focus on just one side of an argument UNLESS the examiner asks you to do so.

Sometimes the examiner will ask for just the advantages or just the disadvantages of a strategy, decision or choice. If this is the case, then just give what you are asked for. For example, if faced with the following question:

Required:

Explain the benefits to ABC Inc. of introducing an internal audit function.

You are being asked only for the advantages and will receive no marks in the exam for discussing disadvantages.

However, if the question asks you to "discuss" or "evaluate" something, then the examiner is usually looking for a balanced answer that considers both:

- Advantages AND disadvantages
- Benefits AND costs
- Good AND bad points

For example:

Required:

Evaluate the impact of the new internal audit function introduced by ABC Inc.

Being able to interpret exam questions like this is an important part of exam technique. I cover it in much more detail in Chapter 12.

4. Prioritise and structure your points

When you have generated several points to discuss in an answer, you need to prioritise these so that you discuss the most important issues first and give them more depth of analysis.

The method I recommend for doing this is as follows. You should have roughed out some points for your answer (preferably using a mind map):

(a) Using a red pen, identify the most important point. This should be the point you make first.

(b) Circle this and write the number '1' next to it.

(c) Then move on to the second most important point, circle this and write '2' next to it.

(d) Continue until you have circled and numbered each point.

[If you are struggling with this process of prioritising your points, I offer some more detailed advice in the next section.]

You can now start to write your answer. You may need to write one or two paragraphs on your most important arguments, but then only a sentence on each of the minor arguments.

When writing your answer, be sure to start each new point with a new paragraph, with a clear space on the page after the previous point. In judging the amount to write and the number of points to make you need to refer to the wording of the question and the number of marks available. I will discuss this in much more detail in Chapter 12, which deals with exam technique for written questions.

Practice Structuring Well-Balanced Arguments

I suggested at the start of this chapter that a good answer needs to contain good points, but also needs to be well structured. I have found that many students struggle with questions that require an evaluation of the strength and weaknesses of something. They manage to generate a good list of points, but then struggle to find a way to structure these points into an answer that flows well. If you find yourself in that position, then here is some advice that may help.

You can usually structure an answer that is balancing positive and negative comments about something in two different ways. A little bit of practice with each approach will teach you which will work best for you in producing an answer that flows well, presents a good argument and is quick and easy to write.

The first approach is to discuss all the positive points first, then all the negative points.

The second approach is to bounce points off each other. For example: "An increase in interest rates will have a positive impact on the return on short term investments, but on the other hand it will increase the cost of borrowing".

Which approach is best? It depends on the context of the question and the points you have come up with. The second approach usually produces an argument that flows better. It also forces you into considering the positive and negative aspects of each issue you examine. However, it will not work if you don't have 'matching pairs' of points to make.

You should practice writing answers using both these approaches and learn to recognise which works best with a given sort of question, and which you feel most comfortable using.

Learning Professional Formatting Requirements

Increasingly examiners are requiring you to answer questions in the form of a professional document, rather than just an essay. Usually there are marks available in the exam for this professional presentation. Some of the marks will be for style – the language you use, but others will be for structure, i.e. demonstrating that you know the stylist difference between a press release and a briefing note. Here is a brief overview of the most common professional formats that are requested in exams:

- Report
- Memo
- Briefing note
- Press release
- Presentation notes
- PowerPoint slide
- Letter

In preparing for your exam you should learn to distinguish between these different formats. You should pay particular attention to the use of language, terms and phrases in each format. It is useful to have some stock phrases to include.

Learn the different headings and common sections. Also, learn to use salutations correctly (yours faithfully/yours sincerely/yours truly).

Practicing Writing Full Answers Under Time Pressure

In the exam you will have to generate ideas and then write out a well-structured and well-balanced answer under time pressure. It is therefore important to practice both of these skills.

When practicing writing answers under exam timing, try to develop a feel for how much you can write in 15 minutes or 30 minutes. This is rather like learning to pace yourself in a long-distance race.

For example, if you know that you are able to write about 500 words in the 15 minutes you have available to answer a question, and you have generated ten points to discuss, then you can recognise that you should spend up to 50 words on each point you make, and no more, otherwise you will run out of time before discussing all of your points.

Using Model Answers Effectively

The model answers that are published with past exam questions are just as important a resource as the questions themselves and you should use them to best effect in your exam preparation.

Always attempt a question first before referring to the model answer. Generating points yourself is an important skill to develop and you will not do this if you read the model answer before you have attempted to generate your own ideas for an answer.

Once you have attempted the question you can turn to the model answer and check for points you missed. The answer may give you new ideas. It may also include points that are missing from your notes. If so, use the model answer to further develop your notes. This is easy to do if you have used mind-maps.

You should be aware that published model answers to exam questions are never definitive. Because of this they are sometimes referred to as 'suggested solutions', a name that leaves room for the possibility of other approaches to answering the question. Examiners will always award you marks for good, relevant points that are not in the published model answer.

Chapter Summary

Writing good answers to written questions is not just a matter of having learned the material. You need to practice and refine your ability to generate good ideas and craft these into well-structured arguments in a range of different styles, from business reports to press releases.

Key Points:

- Practice generating points to discuss, including well balanced arguments

- Practice prioritising and structuring your points into a well-crafted answer

- Ensure that you can write in a range of professional formats, and that you can use the appropriate language, structure and style for each.

- Learn how much you can write in the given time so that you are able to include all the points you have generated within your written answer.

PART 2:

GOOD EXAM PERFORMANCE

Part 1 of this book has been about what you should do in the run up to your exams. However, once you walk into the examination hall, all your hard work and preparation is behind you. From this point on only one thing matters - grabbing as many marks as you can before the invigilator tells you to stop writing!

No matter what you have learned or not learned, what you can remember or cannot remember, once you are in the exam hall you must use everything in your power to maximise your marks.

You don't need to be a perfectionist. You don't need to achieve 100%. Never lose sight of this and never give up.

This is a matter of good exam technique. Exam technique is a different set of skills to the technical knowledge and professional skills you have developed during your preparation period.

It is quite one thing to have a detailed and expert knowledge of the technical content of the exam syllabus, but another to be able to apply that knowledge to maximise your marks in an exam.

It is this second skill that you are going to refine in Part 2 of the book.

CHAPTER 9:
FACING EXAM CHOICES

Most exams present you with some choice between optional questions. In many professional accounting exams, there is one large compulsory question and then a choice of 2 from 3, or 2 from 4 option questions. You are therefore faced with the decision, under exam pressure, of which questions to answer.

Even if there are no optional questions on your exam paper, you still have to choose the order in which you answer the questions. So, let's look at these choices and consider the factors that should influence your decisions.

In What Order Should You Answer Questions?

Unless the instructions on your exam paper demand that you answer all the questions in a specific order, you have three choices:

1. Answer the questions in the order they are presented on the paper

2. Answer your 'strongest' question first, and leave the most difficult question until last

3. Answer the most difficult questions first, whilst you are still fresh.

There is no single right answer to this choice, and I have seen students succeed with all three strategies. What is most important is that you consider this before the exam and go in with a clear strategy. You therefore need to recognise which works best for you.

You may already know, and having read the three choices above, immediately said "Oh, it's option 3 for me". If you are unsure, I would suggest that option 2 is the one that seems to work best for most students. It is psychologically better to start with material you feel more confident about.

Should You Answer All Parts of The Question Together?

Whatever your decision regarding the order in which you answer questions, I recommend that you answer all the parts of a question together. There are two very practical reasons for this.

1. If you jump around between different questions, you will also be jumping around between different syllabus areas and different question scenarios and facts. This will make it much more difficult to focus on the specific details of the question and produce an answer that is specifically tailored to the facts presented. You are likely to waste a lot of time re-reading the question, and you are less likely to develop the focus necessary to produce accurate and insightful answers.

2. Jumping around between different parts of different questions creates an exam answer script that is jumbled, muddled and difficult to mark. Remember that your examiner is human. A jumbled answer script increases the risk of confusing the examiner so that he or she misses or misunderstands which parts of your answers relate to which questions, and therefore increases the risk of you not picking up all the marks you should.

I therefore recommend the following approach:

1. Answer all parts of a question together

2. Start each part of the question on a new page

3. Label each part of each question clearly.

This does not mean that you must answer the parts of a question in order. However, be aware that many exam questions are structured so that the parts follow a logical sequence. It therefore makes sense to answer them in order. For example, consider the following 3-part question, and see how each part logically follows from the previous.

Excerpt from Financial Management Question on Investment Appraisal:

Required:

(a) From the information provided above, construct a cash flow forecast for the proposed investment

(b) Using your cash flow forecast, calculate

    (i)   The payback period

    (ii) The accounting rate of return

    (iii) The net present value

(c) With reference to your calculations in part (a) and part (b), comment on the financial viability of the proposed investment

It would be very difficult to answer the three parts of this question out of sequence. The structure of the question leaves you with little choice but to answer them in order.

Here is a second example:

Excerpt from Management Accounting question on business planning:

Required:

(a) Explain the benefits to a business of producing a cash flow forecast.

(b) From the information provided above, construct a 6-month cash flow forecast for HyperStore Co.

(c) Write a report to the management of HyperStore Co describing the changes they could make to their business operations to improve their cash flows over the next 6 months.

It is possible to answer part (a) of this question at the end, but the sequence offers a logical train of thought. Part (a) asks you to demonstrate your understanding of the benefits of cash flow planning. In part (b) you demonstrate your ability to do cash flow planning. Finally, in part (c) you demonstrate your ability to critically evaluate plans and to write a business report. It is therefore probably better to answer the parts of the question in the order they are set.

How Do You Choose Between Optional Questions?

Many exams have optional questions, and you need to choose which question to answer. Making a good choice is a matter of recognising where your strengths lie. Take a few minutes to read and evaluate each of the option questions. You may be able to make a choice immediately, particularly if it is a computational question. If not, you can test out your ability to answer each question with a quick mind-map. Taking no more than 2 minutes, map out an answer for each option question you are deciding on. Then you can decide – which offers the best potential details to write a full answer?

Chapter Summary

Every exam paper will present you with some choices, from deciding which question to attempt first, to choosing between optional questions. These choices may not be easy in the exam. However, you will be better prepared to make these choices if you have prepared and trained yourself in making these decisions, and you go into the examination hall with a clear strategy.

Key Points:

- Before you enter the examination hall, have a clear strategy for the sequence in which you will attempt questions, according to the exam structure and the topics examined.

- Using this strategy, take time at the start of the exam to review the whole exam paper and to decide on the sequence in which you will answer the questions.

- Answer all parts of a question together and start each question on a new page.

- Label your answers clearly so the examiner has no doubt as to which question and which part you are answering.

- If you are unsure between optional questions, take 2 minutes to mind-map an answer to each. This will help you decide.

CHAPTER 10:
SIX STEPS TO ANSWERING EXAM QUESTIONS

In the exam you will be under time pressure. You therefore need a good technique for quickly and efficiently reading through exam questions and extracting the information you need in order to write a good answer.

Based upon many years of coaching accounting students, I have devised the following 6 step approach to effectively answering an exam question whilst under time pressure.

Step 1 – read the requirements first

When you first turn to a question go straight to the end of that question and read the requirements section. This should be easy to find as it will be clearly labelled with a heading "required" or "requirements".

Whilst reading through the requirements you should be picking up two important pieces of information:

(a) What syllabus area(s) the question is testing.

(b) What the examiner wants you to do (e.g. write a report; complete a tax calculation; prepare a consolidated balance sheet).

By reading the requirements first you immediately get an understanding of what the question is about. You will be up against time pressure in the exam and so you want to get to grips with the question as quickly as possible.

Quite often there will be multiple requirements within one question. Unless you read these carefully it is easy to miss some of these requirements and therefore lose valuable marks. For example, here is a typical 3-part question:

Required:

(a) Identify the objectives of working capital management and discuss the conflicts that may arise between them.

(b) Calculate the cost of the current inventory ordering policy and determine the savings that could be made by using the economic order quantity model.

(c) Discuss the ways in which the business could improve the management of accounts receivable.

Although there are three parts to this question, if you read the requirements carefully you will see that there are actually five separate requirements:

1. identify the objectives…..

2. discuss the conflicts…..

3. calculate the cost…..

4. determine the savings…..

5. discuss the ways…..

You can be certain that marks will be allocated to each of these 5 tasks and therefore if you miss one or more you will be throwing those marks away.

Understanding The 'Action Words'

When reading the question requirement, make a careful note of the 'action words', i.e. what the examiner is asking you to do. For example, a question may ask you to describe, to evaluate or to explain. What is the difference between these actions, and how do they change what you write in your answer? I will look at this issue in more detail in Chapter 12 (Answering written questions)

Allocating Time to Each Part of The Question

Not only must you manage your time carefully across questions, you must also manage your time between parts of a question. When reading the requirements, note how many marks are allocated to each part and use this as a guide to how much time you should spend on each part. Remember that if your exam is 2 hours long, that is 120 minutes. This means that each mark is worth 1.2 minutes. If the exam is 3 hours long (180 minutes) each mark is worth 1.8 minutes. You also need to factor in the time you need to read the question and plan the answer.

Step 2 – read the body of the question

Once you have read the requirements you know what the question is about and what the examiner is asking you to do. You are now able to engage in what I call an "intelligent reading" of the question scenario and information.

You should now read through the entire question. You can now pick out information from the question in full knowledge of what you are required to do with that information.

It is important that before putting pen to paper you read through the whole question and all the requirements. This is particularly important if the question has multiple sections and requirements. I emphasise this because as an examiner I have on many occasions found that students read only the first part of the question before starting to write. After answering the first part they then read the next part and realise that the answer they have just written includes points that they should have made in the second or third part of the question.

Step 3 – underline, highlight and make margin notes

As you read through the body of the question you should pick out all the information and details that will be important to your answer.

I therefore recommend that you either use a highlighter pen or underline key points on the exam paper. For each piece of information that you are given in the question ask yourself:

- why have I been given this information?

- How should I be using this information in my answer?

Make notes in the margin. Even if it is a guess at this stage, it is better to make the note and realise later you are wrong, than to forget the idea that occurred to you as you read the question.

Step 4 – write your answer

Now you can start to write your answer to the question. I have set out more details about how to approach answering different types of questions in later chapters. Chapter 11 covers numerical questions and Chapter 12 covers written questions.

Attempt as much of the question as you can in the time available and only in the time available. Time management is essential. Give it your best shot, but do not be upset if you do not complete the whole question in the time available. This does not mean that you will have failed this question. As soon as you start writing an answer you start picking up marks. So do as much as you can in the time available and keep an eye on the time.

I suggest that whilst writing your answer you periodically refer back to the requirements of the question. As previously discussed, you will find that many exam questions are quite complex and have multiple parts or multiple requirements. It is easy to get engrossed in the question and forget to address one or more of the requirements. You will be throwing away marks if you do so.

Also, check the requirements again to ensure that your answer is addressing the question asked. Some candidates go off at a tangent and end up writing about something different to what the examiner asked for. Sadly, I have seen this many times. I call it "question drift". The candidate drifts away from the set question to one they thought was asked, or one they find easier to answer (the question they wish the examiner had asked!).

Step 5 - attempt all parts of the question

You must attempt all parts of the question. By managing your time effectively, you should allow yourself time to attempt every part of every question.

But what if you come to a part of a question and you don't know the answer? You may well ask "how can I answer a question if I don't know the answer?" My response is that there is usually something you can write to try and grab another mark. This must be your mindset throughout the whole exam: how can I squeeze another mark out of this question? Never give up.

Think of it like this: the examiner cannot award you a mark for something you have not written. If you submit a blank page you give the examiner no option other than to award zero marks. However, if you write something, there is a chance that you may pick up some marks for it. You may not, but at least you have given yourself a chance.

Imagine that you are attempting a financial management question that requires you to calculate the cost of equity of a geared company. You may not know how to do some part of this calculation. For example, you may not be able to work out the dividend growth rate from the information presented in the question. But that should not stop you from demonstrating that you do have some understanding of calculating cost of equity. You can present a formula and insert as many the figures as you are able to. You could even write in your answer that you are unable to calculate the growth rate but are assuming it to be 3% in order to complete the calculation.

You may be fully aware that your answer is incorrect, but at least you are demonstrating to the examiner that you know what is being asked of you and you have an understanding of the techniques involved, even if you are not able to come to exactly the right answer.

As I have already said, this may not get you any marks, but on the other hand it just may get some marks for demonstrating an understanding of approach and technique. This is better than writing nothing, which will guarantee that you get no marks.

Step 6 - never run over your time limit

You must avoid the temptation to run over on time on a question because you have not finished it and you believe that you can. It is so easy to say to yourself "just another 5 minutes and I will finish this". The problem is that this extra 5 minutes may become 10 minutes, and that is 10 minutes that should be spent on the next question.

You will pick up more marks in the first 10 minutes that you spend on a question than in the last 10 minutes that you spend on that question. The first few marks are always easier to pick up than the last few marks.

You therefore need to get out of the mindset of being a perfectionist and get into the mindset of being a mark grabber. You are in the exam to grab marks, not to demonstrate that you are a perfectionist. Believe me, if you start but do not finish every question you will pick up more marks than if you write a brilliant answer to some questions but fail to answer all questions because you have run out of time.

As an examiner I frequently mark exam papers that have brilliant answers to the first question. I read page after page of detailed analysis and insight. The candidate clearly has a detailed and brilliant knowledge of the subject. The candidate may even gain full marks on this question. But then I find that for the remaining questions all the candidate has had time to produce is an outline set of notes that pick up very few marks. The candidate fails. Do not be this candidate. Manage your time.

Chapter Summary

Good exam technique is largely about being able to process a lot of information and take a systematic approach to answering questions whilst under time pressure. The six-step approach to answering exam questions that is set out in this chapter will substantially improve your exam technique.

Key Points:

The six-step approach to answering exam questions is:

- Read the requirements
- Read the body of the question
- Underline, highlight and make notes
- Write your answer
- Attempt all parts of all questions
- Never run over on your time limit

CHAPTER 11:
ANSWERING NUMERICAL QUESTIONS

In the previous chapter I gave you a 6-step approach to answering exam questions. This approach applies to both written and computational questions. However, there are obviously significant differences between answering written and numerical questions.

In this chapter I will therefore focus on the issues that are specific to answering numerical questions.

Recognise the 2 Types of Numerical Question

Most computational exam questions fall into one of two types. This is a very broad generalisation, but it is a distinction that is helpful in preparing yourself to answer such questions.

Type 1 questions

The first type of question requires you to perform tasks that you should already be familiar with. However, the application can be demanding. With this type of question, you know what to do, but the execution is difficult.

Examples of this type of question include:

- preparation of a set of accounts from a trial balance

- preparation of consolidated accounts

- preparation of a tax return or tax statement

- calculation of net present value or other investment appraisal techniques

- preparing a management accounting costing statement

- preparing a variance analysis

With all these types of question you know exactly what you need to be doing, but the execution of some calculations may be complex and deriving the information you need may be difficult.

Type 2 questions

The second type of question is a novel application or idea based upon some aspect of the syllabus. With this type of question, you must recognise what theories or models from the syllabus are applicable to the scenario you are given. This may not be immediately obvious or straightforward. In some cases, there may be no single right answer or right approach to arriving at an answer. You must use your judgement to decide what aspect of the syllabus you are going to apply to answering the question.

Most students regard the type 2 question as being the most difficult. This is because the question does not have an obvious procedure or formula to follow, and it is easy to 'miss the point' of the question.

However, type 1 questions can sometimes be deceptive. You may know what the question is about, for example, producing a set of consolidated financial statements, but the details of the question may be very complex. Do not automatically assume that a type 1 question will be the easy option. Sometimes with a type 2 question the biggest challenge is figuring out the right approach. Once you have done that, the question may be relatively easy to answer.

Show Your Workings

For any computational question, always show your workings. There are three very good reasons for doing this:

- Firstly, there will be marks available for your workings. Even if you get the answer wrong you can still pick up marks by demonstrating your understanding of the principles of what you are doing through your workings. In the heat of an exam it is very easy to make a silly arithmetic mistake. If you set out your workings clearly and the examiner can see that you have understood the principles but have made an arithmetic mistake, then you will still be awarded some marks.

- Secondly, setting out your workings forces you to be more systematic in your approach to the question. This means that you are less likely to make a mistake then if you simply punch lots of numbers into your calculator and then write down the answer.

- Thirdly, if you do make a mistake, it will be much easier for you to go over your answer and spot where you went wrong if you have set out clear and systematic workings.

Rounding

The issue of rounding is probably the one I get most queries about from students. The two questions that I am frequently asked are:

1. when should I round? and

2. what level of rounding is appropriate?

When Should You Round?

The answer to the first question is easy. You should round as late as possible. The reason for this is simple. If you round too early, then your rounding can be compounded in later calculations so that your answer will be inaccurate.

Example: Rounding as late as possible

In a management accounting question, you are calculating a product cost. You calculate the fixed overhead absorption rate as $17.5658 per hour and production requires 10,000 hours of chargeable work.

If you multiply the unrounded absorption rate you get the fixed overhead charge of $175,658

However, if you firstly round your fixed overhead absorption rate to $17.57 and then multiply by the 10,000 hours, you get a fixed overhead charge of $175,700, which is $42 different.

Your rounding of the overhead absorption rate has been multiplied 10,000 times which magnifies it greatly. If the calculation then requires this fixed overhead cost to be added to direct costs and multiplied by a profit mark-up to calculate the price, then the rounding differences will be magnified even further.

You should therefore work with unrounded figures as far as possible - right up to the final calculation.

What Level of Rounding is Appropriate?

In deciding on the level of rounding you should firstly look for guidance from the examiner. In many computational questions the examiner provides guidance in the requirements section. For example: "calculate your answer to 2 decimal places".

If no such guidance is provided, then you should round in a way that is appropriate to the context of the question. Here are a some of illustrations:

Using context as a guide to rounding: Example 1

In a financial accounting exam, you may be required to calculate ratios such as inventory holding period, trade receivables collection period or trade payables payment period. These ratios provide an answer that is usually expressed as a number of days. For example, the trade receivables collection period may be 42 days. If you are calculating an answer in terms of number of days, then I question the value of presenting an answer to several decimal points. In fact, I would suggest that the most appropriate rounding would be to the nearest day. Therefore, a calculation of 41.629 would be rounded to 42 days.

What if you calculate the trade receivables collection period as 38.43 days? You could round it down to 38 days. On the other hand, because the answer actually exceeds 38 days, there is an argument that you should round it up to 39 days. In either case you should show your original calculation (38.43) before presenting your rounded answer. In this way the examiner can clearly see the outcome of your computation and the way that you have rounded this as a matter of interpretation. It is also worth adding a quick note that justifies your rounding to the examiner.

Using context as a guide to rounding: Example 2

Imagine that in a management accounting exam you are required to calculate a selling price. As a selling price is usually given in a unit of currency, then it makes little sense to provide an answer to the fraction of a unit. For example, imagine that you calculate the selling price as $128.63749. It is reasonable to round this answer to $128.64, as that is the nearest actual price that could be charged.

When Performing Calculations, Write Your Answer In 3 Steps

You should always use a systematic approach when performing calculations. As I have already pointed out, there are benefits in writing out your calculations clearly and showing your workings. You will earn marks for your workings, you are less likely to make mistakes and it is easier to spot any mistakes you have made.

I therefore recommend the following 3-step approach to writing out calculations:

1. Set out the formula

2. Add numbers to the formula

3. Reduce, rearrange and solve the formula to find your answer.

Here is an example of these 3 steps applied to a question. This example uses the calculation of inventory holding period:

Step 1: Write out the formula

Inventory holding period (in days) = (Average inventory/Cost of Sales) x 365

Step 2: Add numbers to the formula

Inventory holding period (in days) = ($18.3m/£140m) x 365

Step 3: Reduce, rearrange and solve

Inventory holding period (in days) = 0.130714285 x 365

Inventory holding period (in days) = 47.71 days

Rounded up to the nearest day = 48 days

Recognising Implausible Answers

It is easy to make arithmetic mistakes when you are under pressure in an exam. However, you can develop the habit of checking for and recognising implausible answers. In many cases this is quite easy to do. Here are some examples of how you can do this:

Implausible answers example 1

I once marked an exam paper which required candidates to calculate and comment upon the gross profit margin of a business. One candidate became confused between $ thousands and $ millions and calculated the gross profit margin as 3000%. At that point the candidate should have recognised the implausibility of this answer. However, this candidate unfortunately went on to write several paragraphs about the outstanding performance of the business. If this candidate had simply taken a (metaphorical) step back from their workings, they would have seen that a gross profit margin of 3000% must mean an error in the calculation.

Implausible answers example 2

When calculating the net present value (NPV) of a cash flow, the higher the discount rate you apply, the lower the NPV of the cash flow. Therefore, if you have a question in which you have already calculated the net present value at one discount rate and then perform the calculation again at a higher discount rate, you should expect your answer to be lower. You do not know exactly what the answer should be, and you will not necessarily pick up all mistakes, but you should recognise that if you increase the discount rate and arrive at a higher NPV then you have made some mistake.

Implausible answers example 3

Another example is the calculation of weighted average cost of capital (WACC) on a financial management paper. Usually, in performing a WACC calculation, you must firstly calculate the cost of equity (Ke) and then the cost of debt (Kd) and then perform a weighted average calculation to arrive at the WACC. In performing this calculation, you should be mindful of the fact that the WACC is an arithmetic average and therefore should have a value that lies between Ke and Kd. Whether it is closer to Ke or Kd will depend on the relative market value of debt and equity and you can use these to get a feel of the rough value of WACC before you even start to calculate it. If you arrive at a WACC that is higher than Ke or lower than Kd, then you should recheck your workings as this would be highly unlikely for a calculation of an average.

These are simple but powerful examples of how you can be mindful of what you are doing when performing calculations and thereby pick up on mistakes.

Another important way you can pick up errors in your calculations is by relating your answers to the context of the question. Here is an example from a management accounting exam paper:

Implausible answers example 4

A management accounting exam question provides you with the information necessary to calculate the cost per unit of an item. The question requirement is as follows:

(a) Calculate the price per unit that will be charged using total costing with a profit mark-up of 25%.

(b) A rival manufacturer offers a similar product at a price of $60 per item. Explain how the technique of target costing could be used to help establish a price that is in line with that of the competitor.

If you have followed my advice in Chapter 10 and read all parts of the requirement of the question before starting to answer, you will see that the wording of part (b) implies that the answer to part (a) is higher than $60. If the answer to part (a) were less than $60, then part (b) of the question would make less sense.

Therefore, you can use the information and requirements of part (b) as a guide to what price you should be arriving at in part (a). Obviously, it will not give you the exact answer, but common sense should suggest that the answer will be more than $60, but definitely not hugely more, or again the question would not make sense.

Chapter Summary

Answering numerical exam questions requires a systematic approach. The 6-step approach set out in Chapter 10 applies equally to computational and written questions, but there are some issues and skills that are specific to computational questions. This chapter has looked in some detail at these skills and the issues that frequently challenge candidates.

Key Points:

- Always show your workings when performing calculations

- Round as late as possible

- Round numbers in a way that makes sense within the context of the question

- Follow a clear 3-step process when writing out calculations using formulae

- Check your numerical answers for reasonableness.

CHAPTER 12:
ANSWERING WRITTEN QUESTIONS

Throughout my work as a tutor I have found that many accounting students dislike written exam questions. They feel more comfortable with numbers and prefer answering numerical questions.

If this describes you, then you need to accept that you cannot avoid written questions. Some exams in accounting courses such as law, business strategy or business ethics may be totally written. However, even exams that are predominantly computational will have sections that require written answers. As you progress to more advanced level exams, even those subjects that are traditionally regarded as being highly numeric will have a higher written content, as you are tested on issues of interpretation, analysis and professional judgement.

It is therefore important that you are able to present answers to all types of written questions, whether long or short, in a systematic way that will maximise the number of marks that you earn in your exam.

Understand Different 'Action' Words

All written questions are not stylistically the same and the technique for writing the best possible answer will vary with different types of question. For example, a 40-mark question that requires you to write a detailed business analysis report requires a different approach to a 10-mark question that requires you to evaluate the results of an investment appraisal calculation.

The starting point for recognising how to approach a written question is to develop a good understanding of the different verbs used in the requirements. I call these verbs the 'call to action'. The examiner may ask you to: 'describe', 'explain' or 'evaluate'. It is important that you understand the difference between these verbs and the implication they have for the type of answer you need to write. Here are some of the most common verbs used by examiners, together with my suggestion of what this means for a written answer:

Advise: Provide the facts of a situation and counsel on an appropriate course of action. E.g. "Advise the board on the most appropriate accounting treatment of the asset disposal".

Analyse: Examine something in detail; break it into its component parts. E.g. "Using a SWOT framework, analyse the current financial position of the organisation".

Assess: Evaluate the nature, ability, or quality of something. E.g. "Assess the financial viability of the proposed investment".

Categorise: Place items into defined classes or divisions. E.g. "Categorise the following costs as either fixed or variable".

Compare: [Often this is expressed as "Compare and Contrast"] Show the similarities and differences between. E.g. "Compare and contrast the impact on profit of the different accounting treatments".

Comment: Explain and evaluate. E.g. "Comment on the helpfulness on an internal rate of return calculation to evaluate this proposal".

Critique Set out the good and bad (or positive and negative) aspects of something. Often this is expressed as "Critically evaluate". E.g. "Critically evaluate the argument that dividends should always be maximised".

Define: Give the exact meaning of. E.g. "Define a Finance Lease"

Describe: Set out the key features, procedure or steps of something. E.g. "Describe how you would estimate the discount rate for calculating the NPV of the proposed investment".

Discuss: Set out and evaluate the key features of something. E.g. "Discuss the benefits to the company of introducing an internal audit function".

Distinguish: Show the differences between two or more things. E.g. "Distinguish between an operating lease and a finance lease".

Evaluate: Assess the value of (usually by setting out the good and bad aspects). E.g.

"Evaluate the company's use of current weighted average cost of capital as the discount rate for the investment appraisal calculation".

Examine: Inspect something thoroughly in order to determine its nature or condition. E.g. "Examine the arguments put forward by the two company directors".

Explain: Make something clear or state its meaning. E.g. "Explain what is meant by the time value of money".

Identify: Establish what something is. E.g. "Identify the main factors which contributed to the Stock market crash"

Illustrate: Use an example to describe or explain. E.g. "Illustrate how the adoption of International Accounting Standards would impact the company's balance sheet".

Interpret: Explain the meaning of something. E.g. "Interpret the financial ratios set out in the annual report".

List: Simply set out the features in a list. Beware of writing too much, such that your 'list' becomes 'describe' or 'explain'. E.g. "List the main assumption underpinning the breakeven calculation".

Propose: Put forward a plan or suggestion for

consideration. E.g. "Propose the means of charge-out that would be appropriate for the parent company to debit subsidiaries for their capital employed".

Recommend: Advise on a course of action. E.g. "Recommend an action plan that will incorporate the growth aspirations of the different directors".

State: Express clearly the details or facts of something. E.g. "State the factors that allowed the fraud to occur".

Suggest: Put something forward for consideration. E.g. "Suggest four changes to the management accounting system that might have a positive impact on cultural attitudes and behaviour".

This list is not exhaustive, but it sets out the most common 'calls to action' found in written questions. One of the most important things to learn is how much you need to write in response to each of these calls to action. For example, 'list' requires just that – a list. Do not waste time writing more. However, 'explain' requires you to write more. If you are asked to 'explain the factors…', then simply listing them is not enough. You need to write a sentence or two about each one. But if you are asked to 'evaluate', 'examine' or 'analyse', then you will need to write more than just a sentence on each. This may require a full paragraph or more on each point. This issue of how much to write is extremely important and I therefore discuss it in more detail later in this chapter.

Brainstorming and Mind-Mapping an Answer

You cannot write an answer if you have nothing to write about. Therefore, your priority in answering a written question is brainstorming ideas.

Brainstorming is a method of producing creative ideas through a short but intensive burst of free thinking. You should take 2 or 3 minutes to generate as many ideas as possible, no matter how unusual they may seem. Do not analyse or criticise the ideas at this point, but rather let them flow freely. You can filter and sort them later.

Ask yourself what ideas, theories or models from syllabus might be relevant to the question. Remember that the exam is a test of your knowledge and understanding of the syllabus, so the syllabus should be the first place you turn to for inspiration. For example, if a question in a financial strategy exam asks you to discuss how a firm might achieve growth over the next 5 years, you should recognise that a model such as Ansoff's growth vector matrix could be relevant. Not only will this model help you structure and shape your answer, it will also help you generate ideas by systematically considering each of the vectors in the model.

Apply Your Answer to The Scenario

Always tailor your answer to be relevant to the facts given in the question. The examiner does not want to read a series of generalised or contrived points that are not relevant to the scenario they have given you.

If a part of the model you are applying is not relevant to the answer, don't use it. If a point you have thought of is not relevant, don't include it. Prioritise the points you make into a logical sequence. Be sure to write about the most important points first.

How Much Should You Write?

A question that I am frequently asked by accounting students is "How much do I need to write?" This depends on two factors: The number of marks available and the wording of the question. You need to look at both in combination.

For example, a question carrying 12 marks might ask you to "Identify" the assumptions underlying a breakeven analysis calculation you have just performed. To "identify" you don't need to write too much on each point you make. One short sentence will suffice. It would be reasonable to assume that only 1 mark is available for each comment made. You therefore need to write 12 distinct points to get the full marks.

However, if the question requires you to "discuss" the assumptions, this needs more than one sentence on each point for an adequate answer. You need to write 2 or 3 sentences on each. More marks will be available for each point you make, so you would need to discuss 4-6 distinct points to get full marks.

If the question asks you to "evaluate" then you

should identify and write about both good and bad aspects of the assumptions. You need to give a balanced answer. It would be reasonable to assume that of the total 12 marks, 6 will be awarded for identifying positives and 6 for negatives. A well-balanced answer should therefore contain 3 or 4 comments about good aspects, and 3 or 4 about the bad.

The amount you need to write on each point you make will depend upon the nature of the 'call to action'. More marks will be available for each point you make if the requirement is more complex. This principle, together with the total number of marks available should act as your guide to how much to write.

Laying Out Your Answer to Maximise Marks

On your exam answer script, you should present your answers in a way that makes it easy for the examiner to award you marks. I am now not referring to what you write, but rather the way that you present it.

Do not skimp on paper. You have paid to sit this exam and have therefore earned the right to use as much paper as you want. This is not the time to be concerned about the environment and reducing the number of trees that are cut down for paper manufacture.

Do not write in the margins that are there for the examiner to use.

Do not cram the end of your answer onto the bottom of the page just to avoid running over onto a new page.

Start each answer in a fresh page.

If appropriate, start each part of each question on a fresh page. There are two advantages to doing this.

- Firstly, there is a clear message to the examiner that you are starting a new question or part of the question.

- Secondly, it is easier for the examiner to read. By breaking your answer down into short sections and leaving clear (blank) spaces between sections, you present an answer that is easier to read and follow.

If possible, try and answer each part of the question together. You do not necessarily have to answer them in the order that they are presented (e.g. A, B, C etc), but if you do answer them out of order, be sure to label each section clearly so there is no ambiguity as to which part of which question you are answering.

Lay out your answers in a way that makes it easy for the examiner to identify how many distinct points you are making. For example, if you have generated eight ideas to write about, structure your answer into eight separate paragraphs, each covering a distinct point. Setting out your answer like this makes it easier for the examiner to recognise that you have written about eight distinct ideas. The examiner does not need to hunt within a solid block of text to try and find each point.

The examiner should not have to read through long blocks of writing trying to evaluate whether you are still discussing the same point or are now moving on to a new one. It is a basic convention of writing that a new paragraph signals a new idea. Use this to your advantage. If you write eight paragraphs, each separated by a space, it signals that you have presented eight distinct ideas and therefore deserve the marks for eight distinct ideas.

Of course, your eight paragraphs must contain separate, well written ideas. If they do not, you will not earn eight marks. Examiners are not stupid and will not be fooled by an answer that is well laid out but lacks substance. The point here is not to try and trick the examiner into giving you marks that are not deserved. Rather, it is about making it perfectly clear to the examiner that you actually have made eight good points. If you write one long solid block of text with no breaks, there is a risk that the examiner will not be able to identify all eight distinct points, even if you really have made them. Don't run that risk. Structure your answer to help the examiner, not hinder them.

Presentation

Poor quality handwriting can lose you marks. Put simply, if the examiner cannot read your answer, they cannot award you marks.

Illegible writing is usually the result of rushing to write your answers in an exam. If you suffer from poor quality handwriting, you need to teach yourself to slow down and write more clearly. Writing several pages of illegible scribble will get you less marks than writing a shorter answer that the examiner can actually read.

Most people rarely need to write more than a few lines these days, as most written communication is electronic or is typed. This means that many exam candidates are not in the habit of having to write. They are certainly not used to writing intensely for 2 or 3 hours or more. If this is the case for you, then you need to practise writing. Being able to write several pages quickly whilst keeping that writing legible is an important part of your exam preparation.

In Part 1 of this book I suggested that you practice writing out full answers under exam conditions as part of your exam preparation. Writing is a physical activity. Just like any other physical activity, you need to train your body to be able to do it for long periods of time, such as a 2, 3 or 4 hour exam. I hope that you would not enter a half-marathon race without having trained your muscles beforehand. In the same way, you need to train your writing muscles in preparation for the exam.

Gaining Those Professional Marks

Many accounting exams now carry marks that are awarded for professional presentation. Some of these marks will be available for being able to present answers in the form of a professional communications such as a memo, report or press release. Some of the marks will also be available for adopting a tone and writing style that is appropriate to the type of communication used. These professional marks can be easy to pick up if you simply give attention to these two aspects of professional communication.

Ensure that you are familiar with the layout, structure and language of the main forms of professional written communication. This should include:

- A memo
- An internal report to management
- An external consultant's report
- A press release
- A briefing note
- A PowerPoint slide

Be sure that you know the appropriate salutations and sign offs. For example, if writing a professional letter, how would you change the way you address the recipient depending on whether you already know them or not? When do you sign off a letter "Yours sincerely" as opposed to "Yours faithfully"?

I am purposefully not discussing specific examples here, as I am aware that there are cultural differences around the world for such conventions. For example, you may find it more appropriate to sign off a letter with "Yours truly" or some other form. The point I am making is that you must know what is appropriate and probably more importantly, what is not appropriate.

Chapter Summary

Presenting a good answer that will score high marks is about generating relevant ideas and presenting them well. You need to recognise what information is needed and then presenting it in a well-structured and well-balanced way. Recognising what is needed is not just about knowing the syllabus. It is also about understanding the different 'calls to action' used by examiners and responding to them in an appropriate way.

Key Points:

- Recognise that there are a wide range of styles of written question, which require different approaches.

- Understand the different 'calls to action' and how to structure answers in response to them.

- Practice generating ideas

- Practice structuring your ideas into balanced answers that flow well.

- Use models, theories and ideas from the syllabus to help structure and shape your answers, either explicitly or implicitly.

- Keep your answer relevant and focused.

- Learn to write answers of the appropriate length: not too much, not too little.

- Make it easy for your examiner to award you marks

by presenting a well-structured answer that is clearly laid out and well presented.

A FINAL WORD

Throughout this book I have tried to offer straightforward, clear and practical advice. That advice comes from over 20 years of experience as a tutor and an examiner. I have seen the mistakes that students make, both before the exam and in the exam and it breaks my heart to see students fail. This book is my attempt to ensure that you are not one such student.

In this book, I offer no quick fixes or easy solutions. Passing accounting exams requires hard work and dedication. There is no way around that.

My experience of working with students is that the biggest challenge for most is stress. You will be under stress both throughout your studies and revision period, and during the exam. Preparing for and sitting accounting exams is stressful.

Much of what I have set out in this book is aimed at helping you reduce this stress. Some of the techniques are directly aimed at stress reduction. Others will help you reduce your stress indirectly.

Being organised and systematic in your studies and knowing that you have a study schedule in place that will adequately prepare you for the exam, all help make the process less stressful.

I hope you have found this book interesting and I hope you have found it useful.

Good luck in your exams!

ABOUT THE AUTHOR

Dr Simon N Parry BA(Hons), MBA, PhD, BFP, FCA, FHEA

Simon Parry is a Fellow of the Institute of Chartered Accountants in England and Wales (ICAEW, FCA). He started his career in the early 1980's working in the London office of E&Y where he specialised in assurance and corporate recovery. Since then he has worked in various accounting and management roles in practice, industry and the public sector.

Over the last 20 years Simon has taught professional accounting courses for ACCA, CIMA, ICAEW, CIPD, CIM and IRRV together with academic courses for Business, Accounting and MBA students. He has been the Chief External Examiner for the ACCA, a member of the ICAEW Exam Review Board, and the accounting examiner for the IRRV. He has written study texts and teaching material for several universities and professional bodies and is co-author of the bestselling book Accounting and Finance for Managers.

Simon has held academic appointments at The University of Wales, The Open University, ESSEC (Paris), The University of Cumbria, Oxford Brookes University, The University of Brighton, The University of Bristol and The University of Newcastle.

Printed in Great Britain
by Amazon

85483086R00078